CONSIDERING
GRACE

PRESBYTERIANS
AND THE
TROUBLES

GLADYS GANIEL AND JAMIE YOHANIS

MERRION
PRESS

First published in 2019 by
Merrion Press
An imprint of Irish Academic Press
10 George's Street
Newbridge
Co. Kildare
Ireland
www.merrionpress.ie

9781785372896 (Paper)
97878537-2902 (Kindle)
9781785372919 (Epub)
9781785372926 (PDF)

British Library Cataloguing in Publication Data
An entry can be found on request

Library of Congress Cataloging in Publication Data
An entry can be found on request

Typeset in ITC New Baskerville 11/15 pt

Cover: *Fire In The Storm*, Ballycastle Beach, Co. Antrim.
(Steven Hanna, NEBO Fine Art)

Contents

Acknowledgements   vii

List of Abbreviations   x

Foreword by Susan McKay   xii

1. Introduction   1

2. Ministers   18

3. Victims   46

4. Security Forces   86

5. Those Affected by Loyalist Paramilitarism   116

6. Emergency Responders and Health Care Workers   128

7. Quiet Peacemakers   155

8. Politicians   194

9. Those who Left Presbyterianism   208

10. Critical Friends   220

11. Concluding Reflections   241

Afterword by Alan McBride   252

Endnotes   258

Bibliography   261

*Appendix: Presbyterian Church in Ireland's 'Vision for
    Society' Statement*   263

Acknowledgements

The Presbyterian Church in Ireland's (PCI) Council for Public Affairs (CPA) 'Dealing with the Past' subgroup conceived the idea for this book and steered it to its completion. The subgroup was chaired by Rev. Tony Davidson. The CPA was chaired by Very Rev. Norman Hamilton until mid-2019 and by Rev. Daniel Kane thereafter; its members are Rev. Bill Addley, Catherine Bell, Sam Pollock and Valerie Stewart. Over the course of the project, PCI's Public Affairs Officers Gavin Norris (until 2018) and Karen Jardine (from 2019), and Press Officer Mark Smith, provided invaluable administrative support. The subgroup assisted and commented on the research at every stage of the process, providing vision and perspective.

The project was also overseen by an academic advisory group which included John Alderdice, Stafford Carson, Ian McBride, Duncan Morrow, Ethel White and Gillian Wylie; and a reference group which included Rev. Trevor Gribben, clerk of the General Assembly, and former Moderators Very Revs Stafford Carson, Rob Craig, Trevor Morrow, Charles McMullen, Noble McNeely and Frank Sellar. These groups read drafts of the work-in-progress and provided valuable insights. Very Rev. John Dunlop provided comment on the concluding chapter.

The research was supported by the Irish Government's Department of Foreign Affairs Reconciliation Fund, which funded the employment of Jamie Yohanis as an interviewer and transcriber. The Senator George J. Mitchell Institute for Global Peace, Security and Justice at Queen's University Belfast provided institutional support, facilitated by its director, Hastings Donnan. Queen's academics John Brewer, Katy Hayward and Dirk Schubotz, and Queen's research impact officer Liz Fawcett also aided at key stages of the research. Caroline Clarke transcribed a large portion of the interviews with much care and attention to detail. Joram Tarusarira, director of the Centre for Religion, Conflict and Globalisation at the University of Groningen in the Netherlands, facilitated the volunteer placements of three master's students who assisted with transcribing: Jonathan Barry, Ananda Klopstra and Januschka Schmidt. Madeleine Lerner, a student on Queen's University master's course in Conflict Transformation and Social Justice, also volunteered as a transcriber.

From February to May 2019, Dave Thompson of Confluence Facilitation facilitated a series of three focus groups in six locations. Participants were presented with results of the research and provided feedback on how the material could be shaped into resources to be used in small groups in congregations or presbyteries and for trainee ministers at Union Theological College. These focus groups took place as Gladys Ganiel was completing the book manuscript, helping her to clarify important insights. Dave Thompson also read the full manuscript; his comments were particularly helpful in shaping the concluding reflections.

This book has been wholly written by Gladys Ganiel; the important role of Jamie Yohanis in providing feedback on drafts, and conducting the majority of interviews and transcriptions, warrants his inclusion as co-author.

Conor Graham and Fiona Dunne of Merrion Press were encouraging and supportive during the publication process.

Finally, this book would not have been possible without the willing participation of the interviewees and the Presbyterian ministers who helped us to find them and encouraged them to talk. Our interviewees spoke openly and passionately with us about events and circumstances that tested and re-tested their reserves of faith and fortitude. We hope this book honours their stories and helps us all remember together for a better future.

List of Abbreviations

BB: Boys' Brigade, an interdenominational Christian youth organisation, common in Protestant churches

CPA: Council for Public Affairs of the Presbyterian Church in Ireland

DUP: Democratic Unionist Party

ECONI: Evangelical Contribution on Northern Ireland, a peacebuilding organisation

ICC: Irish Council of Churches, an ecumenical body encompassing most of the island's Protestant churches

ICPP: Irish Churches Peace Project, a peacebuilding initiative of the island's churches, 2013–15

IICM: Irish Inter-Church Meeting, an ecumenical body encompassing most of the island's Protestant churches and the Catholic Church

IRA: Irish Republican Army, a republican paramilitary organisation

ISE: Irish School of Ecumenics

MLA: Member of the Legislative Assembly in Northern Ireland

PCI: Presbyterian Church in Ireland

PSNI: Police Service of Northern Ireland, the police force in Northern Ireland since 2001

RUC: Royal Ulster Constabulary, the police force in Northern Ireland from 1922–2001

SDLP: Social Democratic and Labour Party, a nationalist political party

UDA: Ulster Defence Association, a loyalist paramilitary organisation

UDR: Ulster Defence Regiment, an infantry regiment of the British Army that existed from 1970–92

UUP: Ulster Unionist Party

UVF: Ulster Volunteer Force, a loyalist paramilitary organisation

Foreword

Strangely, it is the small red light of a cigarette burning in the darkness of a graveyard that stays with me as a guide through this compelling book. The man smoking the cigarette is sitting on the grave of his murdered parents, and the person who has been searching for him is his minister, alerted by the man's wife that her husband has gone missing in the night, again. *Considering Grace* is largely preoccupied with examining how the Presbyterian Church of Ireland (PCI) handled the Troubles, and since many of the interviews at its core are with those directly affected by traumatic incidents, there are a lot of glimpses of people struggling with desperate grief – those who could cite, as one person does, Psalm 88: 'You have taken my friends and loved ones from me. Darkness is my closest friend.'

There is a teenage boy crying as he tramps along Ballycastle Beach shouting at God through the roar of the wind and the waves, because he cannot fathom how a God who is meant to represent goodness could have allowed his brother to be killed. There are two little girls following their murdered father's coffin crying out, 'Daddy! Daddy!' Another child is overheard by her mother praying to God to bring her father back 'like Lazarus'. There is a woman whose lamentation for her husband is expressed by absolute silence – she never in her long life after his death mentions his name again. One person says, 'There's no God to let a tragedy like that happen.'

Before the outbreak of the conflict, in 1961, 28 per cent of the NI population were members of the PCI. Inevitably, therefore, many of its flock had to pass through what the psalmist calls 'the valley of the shadow of death'. Among the Presbyterians killed there were members of the security forces, members of loyalist paramilitary groups, and, mostly, ordinary people. The book has searching interviews with people whose faith that their God was with them 'to the very ends of the earth' was deeply challenged, and those who struggled to comfort the bereaved. They include first responders, schoolteachers and ministers. One schoolteacher describes trying to comfort a young girl who was tormented because, after a bomb blast, her friend had asked her to help her search for her little brother. Instead, the frightened child had run away. The schoolteacher had to talk her through it, hoping to persuade her that God would forgive her frailty. A minister states bleakly that there is 'no easy way' to tell someone that a family member has been blown up or shot or abducted. There are many gestures of courage and human solidarity, like the flying of a council flag at half-mast after the sectarian murder of a Catholic, or simply visits to neighbours.

The PCI as an institution will be, and should be, unhappy with much of what Gladys Ganiel and Jamie Yohanis have found. Many people feel that the Church was too timid in the face of the aggressive scorn poured on it by Ian Paisley in his belligerent days as leader of the Free Presbyterians. That there was a failure to offer leadership, or to support those who led in difficult local circumstances. Women are critical of a refusal by the largely male hierarchy to recognise their considerable contribution to the search for reconciliation. One minister describes asking why no Catholic priests had been invited to an 'ecumenical' meeting. There was a silence, and then the conversation resumed as if she had not spoken. The Church needs to pay attention, not least because its flock is deserting it. By 2011, the proportion of NI people who are members had dropped to 15 per cent.

Ganiel and Yohanis take their title from the proposal by one man, who was himself bereaved, that people should 'consider grace', which he defines as 'the hope that Jesus offers ... that there is a possibility of living without bitterness and walking on as somebody who is amazingly and wonderfully free'. The ultimate injustice, after all, was the crucifixion. No one who has contributed to this excellent collection of interviews tries to say that this will be easy, and nor is forgiveness always possible. Plenty will choose, as one woman does, to remain silent during the line in the Lord's Prayer, 'as we forgive those who trespass against us'. The authors conclude that 'grace is difficult, but humanly possible'. This fine book contributes to the literature that tries to enable us to emerge with humanity from the darkness.

Susan McKay
September 2019

CHAPTER 1

Introduction

This book explores how ordinary people responded to the Northern Ireland Troubles. It exposes the devastating impact of violence and its effects on everyday life. It also examines the role of Christian faith for people in the midst of conflict, considering how religion could be both a comfort and a burden.

It is based on interviews with 120 people, mostly Presbyterians, with a variety of experiences. They include ordained ministers, victims, security forces, those affected by loyalist paramilitarism (including ex-combatants), emergency responders and health care workers, quiet peacemakers, politicians, people who left Presbyterianism, and critical friends from outside Presbyterianism.[1] These included fifty women, and seventy-seven people from border counties (including the Republic of Ireland). The heart of the book is stories about how these people, from many walks of life, coped when they found themselves in the midst of the violence and mayhem of the Troubles. While the book focuses on Presbyterians, the stories they tell resonate with wider human experiences of anger, pain and healing. There are stories of faith and doubt, fear and courage, suffering and forgiveness, and division and reconciliation.

The title of the book is inspired by an interview with Rev. Terry Laverty, minister at Portstewart Presbyterian Church. When Terry was a teenager, his brother, who was in the Royal Ulster Constabulary (RUC), was shot dead by the Irish Republican Army (IRA). Reflecting on his struggle to come to terms with his brother's death, he said, 'I want to encourage anybody who is struggling as a result of violence and trauma to *consider grace*, to consider the hope that Jesus offers, to consider that there is a possibility of living without bitterness and walking on as somebody who is amazingly and wonderfully free.'

Grace has been defined as free and unmerited favour, extended to those who do not deserve it. It has also been defined as courteous good will. This book does not offer a technical theological definition of grace. Rather, it tells the stories of people who have considered grace, experienced it, and extended it to others. It also tells the stories of those who, for various reasons, have not. Without commanding others to extend grace, it demonstrates that grace is difficult, but humanly possible. It asks readers to join with Presbyterians in considering grace, reflecting on what grace has looked like in the past, and envisioning what grace could look like in the future.

A July morning in Ballycastle

The morning of 16 July 1972 dawned bright and clear in the North Antrim town of Ballycastle. Fifteen-year-old Terry Laverty was shaken awake by his sister. Terry gazed up into her tear-stained face. 'What's wrong with you? Is it mum?' When Terry was four years old, his father had died of an aortic aneurism, leaving behind a wife and seven children. Terry's first thought was that his mother had died. 'No, it's Robert. He's dead!' Terry shook his head. 'He's *not* dead!' Her tears flowed. 'He is dead, he was shot dead last night by the IRA!'

Robert was just eighteen years old. The four Laverty brothers had shared a bedroom, and as young children Robert and Terry had slept in the same bed. Abandoning a promising engineering career, Robert had joined the RUC only eight months before. He had finished his shift at midnight on 16 July and was still in the RUC station in North Belfast when a call came in about a disturbance at a filling station. The constable due to replace Robert had not yet arrived for work, so he volunteered to attend the scene. As the police vehicle entered the filling station forecourt, the streetlamps went out. It was an IRA ambush. The gunman fired into the vehicle. Robert was struck in the head. He died shortly after in the Mater Hospital.

Still in bed, Terry felt a surge of anger and adrenaline: '*Get me a gun till I shoot someone!*' But instantaneously, words from the Bible came to mind: 'Vengeance is mine; I will repay, says the Lord' (Romans 12.19). He felt another sensation, like warm, soothing oil being poured over his body. He felt it was the 'holy fire' of God's spirit taking away his desire for revenge. Terry believes he experienced the presence of God in those moments. But after the funeral, he felt angry with God and at times even abandoned by Him.

Jean, Terry's mother, had raised her children in Ballycastle Presbyterian Church. Their minister, Rev. Godfrey Brown, accompanied the police sergeant to the Lavertys' home and wakened Jean in the middle of the night to tell her what had happened to her son. Terry searched for comfort in the Bible and at church. 'I was looking for answers and wasn't really finding them.'

Terry also became angry – not at the IRA, nor at local republicans who drove past his house at night, beeping their horns to taunt the family. He was angry with Rev. Ian Paisley, the local MP. One of Terry's cousins told him that he had been speaking with Paisley, who promised to visit Terry's mother. He never did. Whenever Paisley came on the radio or television, Terry was filled with anger about, 'That big man with the big mouth, who couldn't even visit a widow who'd lost her son in the Troubles!' Paisley, founder of the Democratic Unionist Party (DUP) and the Free Presbyterian Church, was viewed by many as a nemesis of Presbyterianism during the Troubles. His figure will loom large throughout this book. But for young Terry, Paisley's oversight was a source of very personal pain.

In the weeks that followed, Terry tramped along Ballycastle Beach, shouting at the God behind the wind and the waves – the God he wasn't sure he believed in. He found himself weeping at the slightest provocation, which was embarrassing for a 15-year-old boy. When he was still struggling with tears ten months after Robert's death, Terry's school principal called him to the office and asked what he would be doing if he were not in school. 'Riding my bike. Golfing. Fishing.' The principal told him to forget school, that he was free to cycle, or golf, or fish, until he got his tears sorted out. Terry said: 'There was no provision in the system for counselling then. But that single act, that gesture of amazing compassion was very important for my healing.' So, Terry pedalled his way through the Glens of Antrim, pausing to get off his bicycle and shout at God. One day on the beach, having shouted at God about the futility of Him 'gathering our tears in a bottle' (Psalm 56.8), Terry went silent. 'I felt these words come into my heart: "Tears are the words the mouth can't speak. Tears are the words of your heart."' He became conscious of the tears of all who were suffering in the Troubles, not just his own.

When he was younger, one of Terry's Sunday School teachers rewarded his pupils with pocket money for memorising Bible verses. Motivated by his desire to buy sweets, Terry had amassed vast knowledge of the scriptures. He recalled Psalm 88: 'You have taken my friends and loved ones from me. Darkness is my closest friend.' He found comfort in these words, understanding them as permission to be angry with God. Terry now believed that God understood his anger – and had been with him all along.

It wasn't until Terry was in his early twenties that he stopped being angry with Paisley. He heard an evangelist preaching who said, 'Forgiveness is important because it's all about *you* being free.' He went home and wrote to Paisley: 'You don't know me and I don't know you, but I've been so angry that you never came to visit my mother. Now I realise that was wrong and I want to ask your forgiveness and tell you I forgive you.' This was the final piece of the puzzle in letting go of his anger. Paisley wrote back, assuring Terry that he had never been asked to visit his mother.

Terry shared these experiences forty-four years after Robert's death. Like so many others who have been bereaved in the Troubles, his memories are still fresh. Whenever Terry hears the Death March, which was played at Robert's funeral, his nostrils fill with the smell of the spices that were used to prepare his brother for burial. He is once again that 15-year-old boy, carrying his brother's coffin. He weeps when he conducts weddings, because

Robert never had the opportunity to enjoy marriage, or
have children of his own. 'The pain never fully goes away,'
he said. 'Although, thank God, my whole family have
been given grace to get through.'

Terry knows his experiences were exceptional. As a
minister, he has met many who have not experienced
healing in any way. He often feels guilty because he can
never fully explain why he received such grace, while
so many others did not. 'I am conscious that there are
people who will read this and say, "Why did God not do
that for me, too, when I experienced hell on earth?"' He
grieves because people who have experienced trauma are
filled with doubt that God exists and intervenes in human
affairs at all. He remembers the difficulties clearly, but is
grateful that the pain of the journey has brought him to
a place where he is not angry anymore; where neither he
nor his family feel like victims.

But Terry sees his story not as a prescription, nor as
a goad to others that they must forgive and move on.
Rather, he presents his story as an invitation. It is the
invitation that is at the heart of this book: to *consider grace.*
Terry says: 'I want to encourage anybody who is struggling
as a result of violence and trauma to *consider grace*; to
consider the hope that Jesus offers, to consider that there
is a possibility of living without bitterness and walking on
as somebody who is amazingly and wonderfully free.'

If religion has been part of the problem, it must be part of the solution

This simple phrase is often used by scholars of religion
and conflict. The idea is that in conflicts where religion
has played a role, peace is more likely if people of faith

are involved in building it. Although the so-called 'two
communities' in Northern Ireland commonly identify
themselves as Protestants and Catholics, many people
refuse to believe that the conflict has had religious
dimensions. We are convinced that a wide body of
scholarship, amassed over many years, demonstrates that
while religion has not been the primary cause of conflict
in Northern Ireland, it has been part of the 'problem'.

In 1986, Steve Bruce, a sociologist at Queen's
University, wrote that 'The Northern Ireland conflict
is a religious conflict.'[2] If taken out of context, Bruce's
conclusion seems absurd. The Troubles were not a holy
war. But Bruce was not arguing that people were fighting
over nuances in Protestant and Catholic doctrine. He
recognised that the violence was fuelled by competing
political allegiances, as well as economic and social
inequalities. Bruce was trying to explain why Rev. Ian
Paisley was so popular within unionism. Paisley seemed
like a throwback to earlier centuries, a crusading preacher-
politician who whipped up Protestant crowds with fiery
anti-Catholic rhetoric. Paisley had created a surprisingly
successful political party, the DUP, which was then the
second-largest party in unionism; not to mention a new
Protestant denomination, the Free Presbyterian Church.
The Free Presbyterian Church had attracted people away
from independent evangelical churches and gospel halls,
as well as from larger denominations like the Presbyterian
Church in Ireland (PCI), the Church of Ireland and the
Methodist Church. Paisley regularly criticised these larger
churches, but he reserved most of his damnation for
PCI. It seemed that Paisley, the son of a Baptist pastor
and a Scottish woman from a Covenanter background,
called his church Free *Presbyterian* as a way of criticising

Northern Ireland's largest and most influential Protestant tradition. Paisley and his followers routinely picketed PCI's annual General Assembly, protesting that the church had become too liberal, too ecumenical, and too sympathetic to the Catholic Church. Rev. Dennis Cooke, a Methodist who wrote a biography of Paisley, put it this way: 'No Protestant church has received more abuse and criticism from Paisley than the Presbyterian Church in Ireland.'[3]

While analysing Paisley's career, Bruce argued that religion mattered more for Protestants than it did for Catholics. In other words, religion was a very important aspect of unionist identity, but was not as important a part of nationalist identity. He wrote: 'This is the only conclusion that makes sense of Ian Paisley's career … [Paisley's] political success can only be understood if one appreciates the central role which *evangelical religion* plays in Ulster unionism.' (author's emphasis)[4] We would add that Northern Ireland's brand of evangelicalism reflects and has been shaped by an older Presbyterian tradition.[5]

In the eighteenth and nineteenth centuries, the evangelical movement swept through Britain, Ireland and North America. Then, as now, evangelicals were best-known for their emphasis on conversion – their insistence that one is not born a Christian but rather must be 'born again' in order to be a true Christian. They believe that being born again gives people a personal relationship with Jesus. Evangelicals also believe that the Bible is the inspired word of God. Many, but not all, insist that the Bible should be understood literally. In the north-east of Ireland, evangelicalism intersected with the existing Protestant traditions, the largest of which was Presbyterianism. Presbyterianism had gained its foothold in Ireland with the arrival of Scottish settlers during the Plantations of the early 1600s. Evangelicalism appealed to people across all Protestant denominations, serving as a unifying force. It informed the ethos of the Orange Order, which was formed in 1795. It helped to quell previous antagonism between Presbyterians and the established Church of Ireland. Presbyterians had been subjected to some of the same penal laws as Catholics – their marriages were not recognised by the state, and they were compelled to pay a tithe to the established church. As relationships among Protestant traditions improved, evangelicals adapted and adopted theological concepts from Presbyterianism. One of the most important of these was the covenant. The idea behind the covenant was that Christians were in committed, covenantal relationships with both God and the state. If the state followed God's laws – including upholding 'right' religion – God would bless it. If it did not, God would curse it. It was Christians' job to monitor the state, ensuring that it followed God's laws and protected 'right' religion. If it did not, Christians were required to resist the state, even violently as a last resort. This covenantal commitment to both God and the state is reflected in the popular slogan 'For God and Ulster'. It is no coincidence that the document that unionists produced to oppose Home Rule in 1912 was called the Ulster Covenant, and that one of the perceived threats of Home Rule was that 'right' religion would be overwhelmed by Catholicism. Hence the unionist slogan: 'Home Rule is Rome Rule.'

So, it is significant that this book's invitation to *consider grace* comes directly from the large and long-standing Presbyterian tradition. Today, Presbyterianism's influence is waning as secularisation gathers pace. Like all Christian denominations, the numbers of Presbyterians have been

declining steadily throughout the Troubles. In the 1961
Census, 29 per cent of the overall population identified as
Presbyterian – by 2011, only 19 per cent did so. PCI's official
membership statistics echo these trends. In 1961, 28 per
cent of the population of Northern Ireland were members
of PCI; by 2011, that had dropped to 15 per cent. Even
so, Northern Ireland is one of the least secular regions
in Europe. It is, without a doubt, the most evangelical-
saturated place in Europe. In 2008, Claire Mitchell and
James Tilley estimated that up to a third of Protestants
could be considered evangelicals.[6] And evangelicalism
remains a major force with Presbyterianism. It is a source
of strength within PCI, providing energy and enthusiasm.
It is also a source of division. PCI struggles to balance
tensions between evangelicals and non-evangelicals. There
are even tensions among evangelicals who disagree with
each other on a range of issues. One of the most significant
of these issues is how to approach peacebuilding – or even
if peacebuilding should be a priority at all.

Considering Grace

The General Assembly of PCI meets once a year over
four days to discuss issues related to the church and
its role in society. Around 1,000 ministers and elders
attend. It is presided over by an elected Moderator, who
serves a one-year term as leader of the denomination. In
2016, the General Assembly agreed a Vision for Society
statement, in which 'We, members of the Presbyterian
Church in Ireland, saved by grace and called by God to
grace-filled relationships ... CONFESS our failure to live
as Biblically faithful Christian peacebuilders ... [and]
AFFIRM Christian peacebuilding to be part of Christian

discipleship.'[7] The General Assembly also agreed to support the research project on which this book is based, addressing the question: 'How did Presbyterians respond to the Troubles?'

A few weeks after the General Assembly, Rev. Tony Davidson, minister in First Armagh and chair of PCI's Council for Public Affairs (CPA) dealing with the past task group, wrote about the Vision for Society statement and the launch of the research project on the Contemporary Christianity blog. One of this book's authors, Gladys Ganiel, read the post. A few weeks after that, she bumped into Rev. Norman Hamilton, who convenes the CPA. Norman is a former Moderator who has retired from ministry at Ballysillan Presbyterian in North Belfast. 'Who is doing the research project?', she asked. Norman confessed, 'We don't know.'

Norman explained that the task group wanted to contribute constructively to societal healing and public discussion about dealing with the past, so they had decided to gather the stories of 100 Presbyterians with a variety of experiences and perspectives, enabling them to tell a wider story about Presbyterian responses to the Troubles than has ever been available. Through these stories, they wanted to recognise that which was good, honourable and even heroic, while at the same time reflecting on the times when Presbyterians failed to be faithful peacemakers. The project appealed to Gladys, a sociologist at Queen's University. She worked with the CPA to secure funding for the research from the Irish Government's Reconciliation Fund. This enabled Queen's to employ the other author, Jamie Yohanis, to help interview Presbyterians.

The most influential book about the role of religion during the Troubles is *Religion, Civil Society and Peace in*

Northern Ireland by John Brewer, a sociologist at Queen's.[8] He argued that the 'institutional' churches, that is denominations like PCI, did not do enough to contribute to peacemaking. Rather, it was people he called 'mavericks', brave clerics and laity acting in small groups, who took the risks needed to bring peace. Some readers will be familiar with the roll call of these outstanding leaders: Frs Alec Reid and Gerry Reynolds at Clonard Monastery; Presbyterian ministers Revs Lesley Carroll, Ray Davey, John Dunlop and Ken Newell; Church of Ireland Archbishop Robin Eames; Fr Michael Hurley SJ and Geraldine Smyth OP at the Irish School of Ecumenics; and Methodist minister Harold Good, among others. Brewer claimed that the institutional churches lacked the courage and conviction to take peace seriously, and even failed to support the individuals who were doing the hard work on the ground.

During the Troubles, church leaders from the four largest denominations often appeared together or issued joint statements condemning violence. Some denominations released statements advocating peace. The Vision for Society statement is the latest in a line of such statements from PCI. The most significant of these was its 1990 Coleraine Declaration, issued after a special meeting of the General Assembly.[9] It was followed by a 1994 Peace Vocation statement. Only a handful of people told us they had been inspired by these statements. Throughout the Troubles, PCI's Church and Government Committee, the precursor to the CPA, produced a series of documents on peace-related issues. But Brewer dismissed these and similar efforts from other denominations as 'speechifying'. Statements were an elaborate form of preaching to the choir, because only a minority of Christians who were already committed to peacemaking heard them. The message barely registered at all with people outside the churches.

When we asked people to evaluate how PCI *as a denomination* had responded to the Troubles, we were usually greeted with silence. People mentioned individuals like Dunlop or Newell, or talked about what their local ministers and congregations had done. But most could not name any initiatives from PCI itself. Only a few ministers and three laypeople mentioned the Coleraine Declaration, Peace Vocation or Vision for Society. Nor did they talk about PCI's Peacemaking Programme, which ran from 2006–9. Their silence revealed a staggering failure of communication between denominational headquarters, ministers and congregations.

Lynda Gould is clerk of session at Knock Presbyterian in East Belfast. A kirk session is the elected board of elders which governs each Presbyterian congregation; the clerk sees to the functioning of the session, conducts correspondence on the session's behalf and is responsible for all official records and documents. Lynda has many years' experience in faith-based peacebuilding in organisations like Evangelical Contribution on Northern Ireland (ECONI) and YouthLink. One of her frustrations is that peacemaking has been compartmentalised to denominational overseeing bodies such as the CPA or to dedicated peace groups within local congregations, making it the priority of a few people rather than mainstreaming it throughout the denomination. Lynda longs for peacebuilding to be at the heart of PCI. But in effect, she said, the establishment of peace groups has marginalised peacebuilding rather than made it a priority.

On the other hand, many Presbyterians do not agree with PCI's peace statements – especially the idea that PCI should confess for failing to be peacemakers. Some Presbyterians also believe PCI has not done enough to help victims. They think it is wrong that some Moderators and groups like the CPA have advocated reconciliation with Catholics without focusing enough on victims.

It is within this complex and complicated religious context that we carried out our research. Neither Gladys nor Jamie are members of PCI, although Gladys attends Fitzroy Presbyterian in South Belfast and Jamie is a committed member of the Belfast Collective, an independent, evangelical congregation in Belfast. We conducted the research according to rigorous academic standards. We were committed to uncovering as full a story as we could, rather than simply telling PCI what we thought it wanted to hear. That meant including people with a range of experiences and perspectives, people from all parts of Northern Ireland and the border counties, and at least fifty women. Most studies of religion in Northern Ireland have focused on clergy and leaders. Although there are ordained female ministers in PCI, their numbers are few and women's experiences of religion have been neglected.

The research was designed in partnership with the task group, which helped identify the categories of interviewees: ministers, victims, security forces, those affected by loyalist paramilitarism (including ex-combatants), emergency responders and health care workers, quiet peacemakers, politicians, people who left Presbyterianism, and critical friends from outside the denomination. The selection of interviewees was also facilitated through the task group. Tony and Norman wrote to every serving minister in

Northern Ireland and the border counties, inviting them to nominate members of their congregation to be interviewed. The task group used their own knowledge to nominate others. All of the interviewees who had left Presbyterianism and the critical friends were nominated by the task group as well as most of the ministers, who were retired or could not be expected to nominate themselves. Participants were offered anonymity and confidentiality, except for public figures like politicians or others whose experiences would make them easily identifiable in their communities. Interviews were conducted between June and December 2017. Participants were aware that while we were researchers from Queen's, we were also speaking with them on behalf of PCI. In effect, they were invited to speak to the church – and the wider society – through us.

But we are also aware that not everyone responded to the invitation. We interviewed Rev. Rodney Beacom, who ministers to four rural congregations in Co. Fermanagh. Beacom served in the RUC during the Troubles, and was injured in an IRA ambush in 1994. He did not become a minister until nearly two decades later. He said:

> When I look at the families in my congregations who are still suffering because of the Troubles, the reality is they feel forgotten and ignored. When [I got the letter] from Tony Davidson, it was a dilemma for me as to what to do. The first question I asked myself was: What are the victims going to benefit from this? Are they going to be listened to? I did talk to a few victims and told them what I had got and what you were looking to do with this. They didn't want to get involved, so I didn't put any names forward, even though I could have because I know that those

people feel as if they've been abandoned by the state, and abandoned to a lesser extent by the church. It's the price they feel they are paying for peace.

In addition to listening to those within its own fold who have felt forgotten and neglected, the project reflects PCI's desire to be heard by those outside the denomination. In 1995, Rev. John Dunlop, a former Moderator and minister at Rosemary Presbyterian in North Belfast, wrote: 'Perhaps what has been hardest to bear is a widespread sense that outside these grieving families, communities and Churches, few people seemed to care. The deep-seated feeling within the Presbyterian community is that the outside world, even that outside world no further away than Britain, never cared, for they mostly never knew or didn't want to know.'[10]

The people we interviewed had diverse experiences and responses to them. But each person was, in their own way, considering grace. We have structured their stories in chapters based on the categories that shaped the research: ministers, victims, security forces, those affected by loyalist paramilitarism, first responders and health care workers, quiet peacemakers, politicians, those who left Presbyterianism and critical friends. People who waived their rights to anonymity and confidentiality are identified throughout by their full names. Those who did not are identified throughout only by a first name, which is a pseudonym. We did not interview equal numbers of people in each category, so the chapters vary in length.[11] The book concludes with a chapter reflecting on the significance of these stories for the present and the future. It introduces 'gracious remembering' as a way forward. Gracious remembering recognises the need to acknowledge suffering, to be self-critical about the past, and to create space for lament and for remembering *for* the future.

As Presbyterians strive to come to terms with their experiences of the Troubles, the Vision for Society statement reminds them that they are 'called by God to grace-filled relationships'. By reflecting on the experiences of its own people, PCI is asking itself what grace-filled relationships could look like today. It is asking itself if it is up to the challenge of considering grace. And it is inviting everyone on this island to join them on this most painful and difficult journey.

CHAPTER 2

Ministers

Presbyterian ministers served in tense border communities dogged by tit-for-tat violence, in estates controlled by loyalist paramilitaries, in urban interface areas, and in predominantly Protestant towns and villages. Their influence was not limited to church members. Their pastoral care extended beyond their own congregations, and people who otherwise never came to church attended the funerals at which they preached. Some ministers became de facto media spokespeople for the wider Protestant community. As we listened to their stories, it became clear that along with police and emergency services workers, ministers were among the first responders to violent events. This was exhausting work that could leave them too emotionally spent for much else. Some ministers felt that peacemaking was their calling, devoting themselves to reconciliation initiatives with Catholics. Others feared that peacemaking would leave them vulnerable to attacks from Rev. Ian Paisley and his Free Presbyterian Church, or from members of the Orange Order in their own congregations. Others recalled the cautionary example of Rev. David Armstrong, whose elders asked him to resign after reaching out to Catholics in his town. To capture the range of experiences, we have organised this chapter thematically: ministers as first responders, preaching, fear of Paisley, David Armstrong and making peace.

Ministers as First Responders

'I cried in a way I never cried in my life, before or since.'

On Remembrance Sunday morning 1987, David Cupples was in his study putting the finishing touches to his sermon. He had been installed as minister in Enniskillen Presbyterian just two months before. 'I was beavering away, preparing the service upstairs at quarter to eleven when I heard this bang.'

The Remembrance Day bomb in Enniskillen is one of the most notorious incidents of the Troubles. Eleven were killed and sixty-three injured in the Irish Republican Army (IRA) blast as they waited at the cenotaph for a service to begin. Six of the dead were from David's congregation.

As the sirens of emergency services began to wail, it became clear that there had been a major incident. David made his way to the church hall in the centre of town. 'Everyone was sitting around the church hall with their mouths open, and there was this deathly silence. I could feel myself physically beginning to crumble. I could feel the level of trauma in the room and I immediately knew I was going to have to deal with an absolutely overwhelming pastoral situation. But I physically looked up and I said: "Lord, I'm making a decision here not to panic. I'm trying to exercise faith." And I felt strength coming back into me.'

Rumours began to filter in about who had died. He went to his church. 'Some people were waiting for the service to begin, believe it or not. I said: "There will be no service this morning."' He visited the hospital, had lunch, and went to the house of a couple whose baby was to have been baptised that morning. 'I went to their home and actually did the baptism, believe it or not.'

There was an evening service scheduled in David's church. 'We allowed the media into the church and they filmed the service. There is footage of me standing in the pulpit announcing the names of the dead and injured and breaking down in tears and trying to gather myself to continue to read out this list of names.'

Then there were the funerals. David was assisted by the Moderator and by previous ministers of the congregation. 'You were working on adrenaline that week. I believe God gave me grace and strength. Anger within me surfaced later. Just on one or two occasions, in the normal course of events, I found myself angry. When I stopped and asked where it was coming from, I realised that it was from that incident.'

After the last funeral, David heard that another member of his congregation, Ronnie Hill, had lapsed into a coma. Ronnie was Enniskillen high school's head teacher and had been at the cenotaph with his Sunday School class. David visited his clerk of session.

> I said to him, 'John, I honestly fear I am about to go over the edge. If a phone call comes through that Ronnie has died, I don't think I can cope with it.' So, John read a psalm and we both knelt down to pray and that's when the healing took place. He prayed, very, very calmly. But when I started to pray, I cried in a way I never cried in my life, before or since. There was just this absolutely enormous reservoir of pain

and sorrow that built up during the course of the week.

Ronnie entered a vegetative state. David visited Ronnie and his wife Noreen twice a week, every week, till the family left the area in 1991. Ronnie never regained consciousness, dying in 2000.

'I was in over my head.'

Russell Birney, the son of a grocer in Lisnaskea, Co. Fermanagh, felt called to minister around the border. In 1973, he submitted his name for the vacancy in Downshire Road, Newry. He was called, and shortly after added the convenorship of the rural congregations of Newtownhamilton and Creggan to his charge. 'Newry was afflicted with bombings and killings of neighbours of mine. Creggan is about a mile from Crossmaglen, which was the cockpit of the rural campaign of the IRA. It was one incident after the other. I had to travel up from Newry along roads, day and night, that were potentially booby trapped for the army.' A rota of men was organised to guard his church in Newry, day and night, 'because there were incidents of churches being attacked and people being attacked coming out of churches'.

On 1 September 1975, Russell got a call 'about an incident in Tullyvallen'. The IRA had opened fire in an Orange Hall. Four men were killed instantly, and a fifth died later of his wounds. Eighty-year-old John Johnston, a member of Russell's Creggan congregation, was among the dead.

That night, Russell visited the families.

I wasn't trained pastorally for an incident like this.
When I came down from Tullyvallen that night, having
visited those homes – I hadn't seen any bodies, I was
just with the relatives – I sat on the edge of my bed
and cried. I saw the children of some of the deceased
and seriously injured. I called in hospital and I had
seen some of them being treated. It was hard at
that time. It was an aspect of ministry that I wasn't
prepared for. I was in over my head, so I had to adapt.

Five months later, two of the guns used in Tullyvallen
were turned on the ten Protestant workmen murdered
in the Kingsmills massacre, just a few miles away. None
of Russell's congregants were killed in Kingsmills, but he
took part in the funerals and provided pastoral support in
the community.

Russell also needed support, which he found in other
local ministers and his congregations. 'They were very dark
days and they demanded a lot of time. My congregation
was very good in allowing me to give that time, because
they were sympathetic in every sense to it.'

'I had to keep it all together for their sake.'

One minister served in both rural and urban areas. He
had members murdered or forced out of their homes
in every location. He recalled the names and manner of
death of many people. 'The Troubles disappointed me.
I felt so sorry that so many lives were lost. Meaningless,
meaningless. You are sitting beside a widow who has
just been told that her husband has been shot dead or
blown to pieces – it's not easy.' Like other ministers, he
had not been trained for this aspect of his job. 'You deal

with it differently in each home. Sometimes you don't say anything. There is nothing to say. What can you say? Except that you are deeply sorry. You sit with them, and weep with them.' He said he 'prayed constantly', and leaned on his wife for support.

> When you got a phone call, you didn't know what you were going to see. That can be quite shattering. So, you prayed that God would give you the strength to cope with this situation. You go to the house. However much you are breaking up inside you have to be in control for their sake. Because they're going to say, 'What are we going to do now?' Even the very practical things of arranging a funeral, the very practical things like there's no wage going to come in at the end of the week. I had to be able to keep it all together for their sake.

'You never hear our stories.'

William Bingham grew up near the border in Markethill, Co. Armagh. One day a bomb in the town centre damaged his home. A few years later, the IRA left a bomb outside his family's house when they couldn't get close enough to detonate it at the police station. William was at school. It destroyed the house, injuring his grandmother, though not seriously.

> We lived through many shootings in our town. I'd have known many people who were killed. The Kingsmills massacre was just six miles down the road. We had a shooting at the Tullyvallen Orange Hall where many Protestants were killed. We were at all

those funerals. At my grandmother's funeral, while we were carrying her remains out of the church, the police came to tell us that a bomb had been planted underneath somebody's car who was a mourner. The whole graveyard had to be evacuated. We did not feel like we were being singled out, but certainly we felt a close affinity with people who were suffering in the Troubles.

From age eight, William felt called to be a minister. After ordination, he received his first call to the congregations of Pomeroy and Sandholes in East Tyrone, another Troubles hot spot. 'I talked it over with my wife, and she was from a similar background to myself. Both of us felt that if God was calling us there, we had nothing to fear.' In his first year, three people in his congregations were murdered and the area endured a series of bomb and mortar attacks.

When a member of his congregation was murdered, William was the first person the police contacted. They wanted him to visit the family first to break the news. William would pray with his wife and then make his way to the home of the bereaved family. 'There is no easy way to break the news that your husband has been blown up, or that your son has been killed or kidnapped.' From that point on, he was at the family's disposal. 'You read and pray with them, and you spend night and day with them. You try not to leave the house at all – 24/7.' William helped plan the funeral, and then conducted it. If the family wanted him to send out a political message at a funeral, he obliged. 'I would have been saying what I thought of the IRA. I would have been saying what I thought of government if they were trying to appease the IRA.'

For William, his pastoral duty of comforting the family included this political element. 'The families were so thankful. There was this real desire to have a voice, to be heard. They would say: you always hear the other side, but you never hear our stories.'

'I was left there very much on my own.'

Roy Neill was minister of First Castlederg, Co. Tyrone, for four decades; and of Killeter, Co. Tyrone, for two decades. A native of Co. Leitrim in the Republic, he felt at home among the farmers on the other side of the border. He had been in Castlederg for fifteen years before the first member of his congregation was murdered, in 1972. There would be eight more. 'Then there were many more murders of other people who weren't members of my church at all. I think there were thirty-one deaths in that area and seventy bombings. The town itself would have been absolutely wrecked on a number of occasions.' Roy kept a scrapbook of the newspaper clippings describing their deaths. 'A lot of them were young families. They were people who served in the security forces; that's why they were targeted. They were hard-working people. They joined up to try and help the country get back to normality again.'

Roy called on the families in the immediate aftermath and continued for years with follow-up visits. It was important for the families that their relatives were not forgotten. Families often paid for plaques or memorials to be placed in the church building, bearing their loved ones' names.

The Moderator assisted Roy with every funeral. Local clergy from the other denominations, Protestant and

Catholic, also supported him. It was still difficult. 'I always felt that I was left there very much on my own, dealing with people. You were back and forth to their homes frequently after these things happened, to see how they were and if there was anything you could help them with.' Roy's health suffered under the strain and he applied twice for early retirement. 'Somehow I endured and fulfilled my full term.' It has been two decades since he retired, but he visits Castlederg occasionally. He is glad the memorials in the church keep people's memories alive. 'When you visit, you might see people who you watched shedding tears at the time of their troubles. You'd meet them again, and the tears would come back to their eyes. We came through a lot together. I would hope that whatever I did, my ministry among them would have helped them.'

Preaching

'The statement prevented retaliation.'

Russell Birney looked out over those gathered in Clarkesbridge Presbyterian. The small church was overflowing with mourners. It was a united service, organised after the murders in Tullyvallen Orange Hall. He read out a statement pledging that there would be no retaliation. It was an agreed statement, which Rev. John Hawthorne of the Reformed Presbyterian Church had helped him write. 'I read out a statement, pleading for peace and that there be no retaliation for this event.' Russell invited those who agreed with the statement to stand. Not everyone stood immediately, so he waited. And waited. And waited – until everyone in the church was on their feet.

During a time marked by tit-for-tat killings, it was a remarkable occasion. 'I've been told subsequently that the statement prevented retaliation because there were people at the service who were determined they were going to avenge. We were speaking for the victims, for those who were wounded, because they were fine people who would not have wanted revenge. There was no tit-for-tat following Tullyvallen Orange Hall.'

'No road is worth a life.'

During his time in Pomeroy and Sandholes, William Bingham was Deputy Grand Chaplain of the Orange Order and County Grand Chaplain of Armagh. He negotiated on behalf of the Orange Order during the most volatile years of Drumcree (1996–8). The Orange Order sought to parade to the Church of Ireland in Drumcree using the Garvaghy Road, which traversed a nationalist area. The run-up to the parade in 1996 and 1997 had been marred by violence and rioting. In the early hours of Sunday 12 July 1998, just hours before Orangemen from throughout Northern Ireland were due to gather at Drumcree, three young boys were murdered in an Ulster Volunteer Force (UVF) firebomb attack at their home in Ballymoney, Co. Antrim. Richard, Mark and Jason Quinn were from a mixed religious background – their mother was Catholic. The murders were understood as sectarian and driven by the tensions around Drumcree.

William was due to preach that morning in an Orange service at his church in Pomeroy. Given his high profile in the negotiations, the media descended en masse. William was as convinced as ever that the Orange Order had a right to parade, but not at any cost.

I spoke without notes because I thought, this has to come from my heart. The text I took was from the book of Micah: 'What does the Lord require of you but to do justly, love mercy, and walk humbly with your God.' I talked about the justice of the cause and the right that we had. Then I said: 'No road is worth a life. Not the life of three little boys. Not the life of anybody. What's happened in Ballymoney is wrong and is to be condemned. And if you're intent on going to Drumcree tonight to cause violence, then go home. Don't come.'

William's words echoed beyond the walls of his rural church. First and Deputy First Ministers David Trimble and Seamus Mallon issued a statement: 'Nothing can be gained from continuing this stand-off. As the Rev. William Bingham said, no road is worth a life and we echo that statement.' Further violence was averted. But William acknowledged that, 'Some felt I had betrayed the cause at Drumcree. Others were glad that it had been said and were very supportive.'

'We must offer forgiveness unconditionally.'

On the day of the Enniskillen bomb, Gordon Wilson, a Methodist whose daughter Marie had been killed, gave an interview in which he said he bore no ill will towards her killers. His words lingered with David Cupples. 'Gordon Wilson's interview created a different atmosphere but polarised opinions over what is forgiveness. Did he have the right to forgive them? What does forgiveness mean? I knew that sooner or later the issue of forgiveness would have to be addressed.' Five weeks after the bomb, David preached on forgiveness. He said then: 'The debate rages in the Christian church about whether you can forgive people before they repent. I believe if we are to follow the example of Jesus, we must offer forgiveness unconditionally. But the person who has committed the injury cannot actually have an experience of forgiveness unless they admit they have done something wrong.'[12]

Fear of Paisley

We did not ask anyone we interviewed about Paisley, but most of the ministers brought him up. They said that the Presbyterian Church in Ireland (PCI) – from its local ministers to the leaders of the denomination – feared Paisley would attract Presbyterians into his Free Presbyterian Church. The result was that PCI became more conservative and less open to peacemaking than it might have been. One put it this way:

> We were under pressure from the Paisleyite faction who would be very quick to say 'Traitor!' Paisley was a great problem for our ministers. A lot of our members were influenced by Paisley. A lot of ministers would have loved to have said and done more but that Paisley threat inhibited them from saying too much, too plainly, too publicly.

Another minister recalled how when Paisley emerged as a public figure in the 1960s, people at first treated him as 'a figure of fun, a relic of another century'. He was only a teenager at the time, but he recalled one 'very decent Presbyterian elder, saying late one night: "I don't agree with his methods, but there is a lot in what he says." And

I should maybe have paid more attention to that at the time.' After he became a minister, he was dismayed at the impact Paisley had on PCI. 'If you were a Presbyterian minister in a small community and you did something that displeased some of your people, then the Paisleyites were in like a shot. You're in a small congregation. The Free Presbyterians are starting up the road. You're not going to do something that's going to see forty families disappear.' In 1980, PCI voted to leave the ecumenical World Council of Churches (WCC). There were concerns that WCC humanitarian aid was being diverted to terrorist groups in Africa. But it is likely that Paisley's anti-ecumenical activism was another factor. This minister continued: 'I think a lot of people within Irish Presbyterianism shared Paisley's basic theology. Did he bring us out of the World Council of Churches? I doubt it. But did he have an influence in that? I think he did.'

Many Presbyterian congregations were bitterly divided in their opinions about Paisley. We spoke to one minister who served in a rural congregation with many members of the Orange Order. 'There were a succession of special services: for the local Orange Lodge, the District Orange Lodge, the Black, etc.' On one occasion, 'one of these firebrands wanted Paisley to conduct the service in my church'. The minister – taking a considerable risk – refused. A man standing nearby said, 'Then we'll just let him speak in the field.' He was met with this pithy retort from another man: 'It's the right place for him!'

David Armstrong

Some ministers said that what had happened to David Armstrong in First Limavady, Co. Londonderry, served as a cautionary tale: anyone who tried to reach out to Catholics would not be welcome in PCI. Just as we did not ask people about Paisley, we did not ask people about Armstrong either – but they wanted to talk about him. We also interviewed him.

David served in Limavady from 1981 to 1985, making a series of reconciliatory gestures towards Catholics. The most widely known were on Christmas Day in 1983 and 1984, when David walked across the street from his church to Christ the King Catholic Church to shake hands with Fr Kevin Mullan. Armstrong and his family received death threats from loyalist paramilitaries, and eventually the elders of his church asked him to resign. He resigned in May 1985 to train for ministry in the Church of England. He later became a Church of Ireland minister in Cork before retiring to Northern Ireland.

First Limavady was David's first post after serving an assistantship in Carrickfergus. He was an evangelical, and he threw himself into his duties. He also became a chaplain in nearby Magilligan prison.

I found there was absolutely no difference in the UVF and IRA prisoners. I couldn't say one was worse than the other. I was in the cells with Catholic prisoners and I was not ever wanting to make them into Prods [Protestants]. There were people writing to me and saying, 'David, it's lovely the way the Catholic prisoners listen to you. I hope you're saving them into the Protestant church.' I was saying, 'No, even though I'm an evangelical Christian, my duty is to love people and not make them into me.' So people felt like you've fallen down in your job for not 'saving' Catholics.

Christ the King Catholic Church was still under construction when David arrived. In October 1981, as it neared completion, it was damaged in a loyalist bomb attack. 'When the roof was restored and the church was opened, the clergy all got invitations. I said I would go. But the replies the priest got: "Dear Mr Priest, regarding the opening of your premises, I will not be going to your Papish house of Satan." That was one of the nicest replies.' David received threatening phone calls and his children were harassed at school. 'They came home with spittle on their faces being told: "Your daddy better not go to the mass house."' David told his congregation he was attending because it was the right thing to do. Some people left his congregation after that. No other Protestant clergy accepted the invitation, but the governor of Magilligan, a former Presbyterian minister, accompanied David.

On Christmas Day 1983, Kevin met David at the door of his church and asked, 'Would you object if I shook hands with your people on Christmas morning coming in to church?' David invited him to greet his people from the front of the church, and Kevin did. When David's service ended, he walked across the road and stood at the back of Kevin's church. The service was about to conclude. Kevin saw him, and asked him to speak from the front. 'When I finished, they burst into applause. They stood and cheered. Old ladies of ninety said, "This is the happiest Christmas we've ever had. We never thought a Protestant minister from across the road would ever be seen in our church."'

On Christmas Day 1984, David and Kevin were set to repeat the goodwill gestures. About forty Free

Presbyterians protested outside David's church. Three were inside among the Presbyterian worshippers. When Kevin went to the front to speak, a Free Presbyterian stood up and accused David of 'treason before God'. There were scuffles in the church. David sighed as he recalled these incidents. 'Saying Happy Christmas – the Free Presbyterians and the Orange Order went absolutely berserk.'

The pressure on David intensified. On a trip to Belfast, he was abducted by loyalist paramilitaries.

> I went through to a back room of an illegal bar and I said something stupid: 'Men, I think you're more frightened of me than I am of you.' But they came to the conclusion that if the fundamentalists want to kill me, let them do it. They didn't accept my outlook but they admired my guts. One of them said they were going to give me twenty minutes to get away.

David finally accepted an invitation from sympathetic clerics in the Church of England to retrain for Anglican ministry. As he was leaving for England, Rev. David Bailie from Bangor West Presbyterian invited him to come as an assistant.

> The police said, 'David, the people who want to kill you will find it easy to get you in Bangor.' I feared that some of my colleagues would say, 'He never really intended to go. It was all a bit of drama.' I didn't want my children to suffer anymore. Now they're pretty proud to say, 'Yes, the Rev David Armstrong is my dad. We can hold our heads high.'

Making Peace

'Maybe another word for faith is risk.'

Ruth Patterson took a deep breath. Along with her elders, she had travelled for a weekend away in an enclosed convent in Dublin. It was the early 1990s, and Ruth's congregation was in Seymour Hill, Dunmurry, in a loyalist estate with a heavy paramilitary presence. One of her elders was an Orangeman. She had not been sure if he would come. As is customary in an enclosed convent, the Sisters sat behind a grille. The Presbyterians sat on the other side. They had just shared their experiences: what it was like to be a Presbyterian elder; what it was like to live in an enclosed Catholic community. They had shared an act of worship, singing together, 'Jesus is Lord, creation's voice proclaims it'. Ruth said, 'Some of my big men were in tears.' They had been served tea, and were talking informally through the grille. Ruth had spotted her Orangeman, conversing animatedly with a nun: 'Their noses were right up against the grille, and both of them were chatting away. It turned out both of them had been born in Derry, and in the discovery of the one beloved birthplace all difference had gone out the window. I just stood there and thought: I am witnessing a little miracle of reconciliation.'

Ruth was the first woman ordained in PCI, in 1976.[13] By the time of this encounter, she had been in her congregation for nearly fourteen years. This little miracle could not have happened on day one.

I do not think any of the denominations were as prophetic or courageous as they could have been during the Troubles. I can understand on one level, especially for clergy who were married and had families. To step out would have been horrendously difficult. But if we couldn't do it, what right have we to ask anybody else to do it? We are meant to be in leadership, you know.

As a young woman, Ruth had been inspired by Rev. Ray Davey, a Presbyterian chaplain at Queen's who founded the ecumenical Corrymeela community in 1965. She believed passionately that Christians of all denominations should work together. But she knew this wouldn't happen overnight. In her first post as an assistant minister in Larne, a predominantly Protestant town, she attended an inter-church clergy meeting. 'Where are all the priests?' she asked the other ministers, all Protestant. 'There was a silence, and they then resumed their conversation as if I hadn't asked anything.'

When Ruth was called to her own congregation, she helped start a praise group among the Protestant churches on the estate. The praise group used songs and prayers inspired by the charismatic movement, which had also made in-roads in Catholicism. She was delighted when some Catholics began to attend. She talked, listened, prayed with people, slowly building relationships. Protestant and Catholic women from the praise group set up a prayer group. Then they set up a clergy group. Then the clergy wanted to exchange pulpits. Ruth asked her elders to vote on whether a priest could preach in their pulpit. Fifteen of the twenty agreed. She didn't go ahead with it, because she wanted everyone on board. A few months later all twenty said yes. 'These steps were big for them.'

Ruth knew that not everyone in the estate was happy with her approach. But she earned the respect of the

paramilitaries. Although not churchgoers, some of the
paramilitaries asked for her support in times of distress.
Ruth did not turn them away. 'Obviously not everybody
would have been happy with what the majority of the
committed people in our congregation were doing. But
nobody left us to join the Free Presbyterians. They all
stayed with it.'

It would have been easier to focus only on her own
flock, tending just to their needs. For Ruth, that would
not have been what it meant to live out her faith. 'In
times of adversity and threat people look to external rules
and regulations and batten down the hatches rather than
stepping out. Maybe another word for faith is *risk*.'

'After that I got very unhappy phone calls.'

Barry was minister in a border town. The windows of his
church were blown out repeatedly in bomb blasts. He
buried members of his congregation. Some members
belonged to the Royal Ulster Constabulary (RUC) and the
Ulster Defence Regiment (UDR). They told him that IRA
men taunted them in the town, letting them know that
they knew who had killed their families and colleagues.
On one occasion, he was asked to take the funeral of a
loyalist paramilitary who was nominally associated with his
congregation.

I said, 'Certainly, I'll do the funeral gladly, but not if
there is paramilitary presence.' A half hour later there
was another call to say that I had not been invited to
take the service, and on no account was I to take the
service. So, another clergyman with known political
associations came and took the service. There were

about fifteen buses parked at the roadside which had transported paramilitaries from Belfast and elsewhere. During the funeral it was said from the pulpit that it was a disgrace that the man's own minister refused to take the service. After that I got very unhappy phone calls, threatening phone calls.

While Barry's wife Sandra remembered the tensions in the town, she also remembered those who quietly built relationships with each other. Women started prayer groups. One evening, a Catholic woman walked into a meeting. There was an Orangeman present, who regarded her suspiciously. Barry recalled,

By the time the Catholic woman had finished praying, the Orangeman had no doubt whatsoever that she was a Christian. You couldn't have prayed the prayer she did if you hadn't been. It was quite the transformation to see his face when he saw she came into enemy territory and prayed as she did. It did him a world of good!

'There were often gun battles on the road,
riots outside the church.'

Husband and wife Patton and Marlene Taylor both served as Presbyterian ministers during the Troubles. In 1985, Marlene was the first mother ordained in PCI. Patton, from Scotland, had been ministering since 1977 in Duncairn Presbyterian in North Belfast. The local Protestant population had largely fled. The church looked directly over the republican New Lodge area. There was an army barracks across the street. Most members of the

congregation commuted from the suburbs. The manse
was adjacent to the church and Patton and Marlene lived
there with their five children. Patton said,

> I consciously chose to go there because it was a
> Presbyterian church in the middle of what was now a
> republican area. There were all kinds of issues around
> that but I went – perhaps with a certain naiveté but
> also with some conviction. I felt that a church in that
> situation ought to have some witness in the immediate
> local community.

Duncairn Presbyterian worked with the nearby Antrim
Road Baptist Church to set up summer schemes for
children and teenagers. Many Catholic children attended.
These activities grew into the 174 Trust, which employed
youth workers and hosted short-term volunteers from
Northern Ireland and around the world. Tony Macauley's
memoir, *Little House on the Peace Line*, tells the story of that
ministry from a youth worker's perspective.[14] Patton said,
'There were often gun battles on the road, riots outside
the church, petrol bombs flying. We had a period where
the congregation had a contract with a local glazier to
come in Mondays and fix the windows that had been
broken in the manse that week.'

Marlene ministered in Cooke Centenary Presbyterian
on the Ormeau Road in South Belfast. 'For me, that was a
release to get out of the manse and to go to a community
that was more mixed.' There were still Troubles-related
deaths in the area. The local clergy fellowship took it in
turns to visit the bereaved, going together in Catholic–
Protestant pairs. Marlene said, 'We felt it was important to
keep a visible presence on the road for a kind of stability.

We wouldn't meet behind closed doors. We would meet in a café, or a community centre, and be seen walking down the road and being together.' Marlene journeyed back and forth across the city through army checkpoints. 'It was particularly difficult to get back into the manse again in the evenings to feed my baby. I had to literally go and face the army to negotiate to get in. If they didn't let me in, I would get in by some way. That was how strong the feeling was that I had to get back in to feed that child.'

The Duncairn ministers and youth workers met every morning to pray. The Taylors hosted evening prayers in their home for their family and the volunteers who lived with them. People in their congregations offered varying degrees of support. Marlene said, 'I think if we hadn't had that group of committed people in the church whom we could have contacted day or night, we wouldn't have made it. We didn't feel supported by the Presbyterian Church as such. No one centrally contacted us during tense periods, and that was hard.'

'The call to ministry was very much about peacemaking.'

Abigail became a minister because she wanted to contribute to peace. 'For me the call to ministry was very much about peacemaking. If the church wasn't going to be doing something about that, then who was going to be doing it?' She grew up in a tense border town where the curtains were drawn in her school's windows during bomb scares. 'Like that was going to save us!' When she was a teen, a Catholic couple she respected was murdered by the notorious Glenanne gang. When she went to church the next Sunday, the murders weren't mentioned at all. 'There was no acknowledgement that it happened. No apology, no nothing, which seemed to me just brutal. Plus, we couldn't go to the chapel for the service because those were the days when Protestants didn't go to mass. You didn't step your foot over a chapel door – you'd have been in big trouble.' Abigail later discovered that members of her congregation were in the Glenanne gang. 'That was shocking. The fact that the church would condemn [loyalist murderers], yet they were sitting among us, they were part of us.'

Abigail's first post was in an urban interface area. 'The Troubles were unavoidable. You would have a baptism and people would turn up at church with their UDA [Ulster Defence Association] or UVF badges on.' In some ways, the urban interface was more open than her border upbringing. There was already an inter-church clergy group. She received invitations from local Catholic priests to speak in their churches, and to become involved in grassroots peacemaking with paramilitaries.

> I'd just arrived from the country, and there was a Catholic priest phoning me. It was scary. Did I consider republicans my enemies? Absolutely. Did I think of those Catholic priests as my enemies? I wouldn't say that. But I wouldn't say I was too sure of them either, at that point. But I believed it to be a Gospel call and a Gospel obligation. That's why I did it.

As a woman, Abigail was perceived as non-threatening. This allowed her to say things and make contacts with people which might not have been possible if she were a man. She remained convinced that Christians in a violent, divided society should be peacemakers. 'For me, faith is spelt "r-i-s-k". If I hadn't been prepared to do those things, and if my congregation hadn't been prepared to do them with me, I don't think we would have been faithful people.'

'I had no fear of the UDA and the UVF.'

Bill Moore grew up on the Shankill Road, the son of a lorry driver and a stitcher. His parents worked hard to send him to the Royal Belfast Academical Institution (Inst). Inst was, he said, a 'snobby' school for a lad from the Shankill. In 1981, he accepted the post in Taughmonagh Presbyterian in South Belfast. It was a place most ministers didn't want to go: a socially disadvantaged estate with a strong UDA and UVF influence. 'I told them I would stay five years – I was there twenty.' Bill loved the people and identified with them due to his own background.

Bill methodically built relationships with people in Taughmonagh. 'I had no fear of the UDA and the UVF on the estate, because I'd visited their parents in hospital and visited them in gaol. I visited their houses, married some of their connections. A generation grew up and had known me.'

These relationships stood Bill in good stead when he felt he should challenge the paramilitaries. In 1991, Catholic taxi driver Harry Conlon was abducted by the UDA and murdered in Taughmonagh.

I put a little cross where he was shot and it disappeared. So, I put a bigger cross in the spot and it disappeared. Then the big cross appeared back and there was written on it: 'Bill Moore, Rot in Hell. Death to all Taigs.' A taxi driver in the estate told me it was women who actually done that. I said, 'It's good to know that it wasn't the real hierarchy of the UDA!'

On another occasion, the UDA 'disciplined' men on the estate who did not have 'approved girlfriends'. In other words, they were dating Catholics. Bill's church committee circulated a flyer that read:

> During the week three young men from Taughmonagh have been shot in the leg by Taughmonagh UDA and it is rumoured that they plan to do the same to certain others. Our lives and the lives of our children are now under threat. The church is organising a peaceful protest against these shootings. The protest is not against the UDA, but against illegal punishments.

The letter encouraged people on the estate to give information to the police. The UDA wrote a letter back that said: 'If you think the police are friends of Taughmonagh, you're living on a different planet.'

After that, Bill's church was daubed with graffiti and an arson attempt destroyed the church kitchen. It was rumoured he would leave the estate, but Bill believed God wanted him there – and that there were people on the estate who wanted him there, too.

> In one public meeting, a UDA man attacked me and one wee woman stood up and she says, 'Now, keep Bill around because when I got my house burgled he came round and he gave me money and you lot didn't do that!' The UDA man said, 'I actually like Bill Moore, it's just the things he says I don't like!'

'He's still alive.'

Bangor West was established as a new congregation in 1961. David Bailie was there from the beginning. A predominantly Protestant town, Bangor did not experience the Troubles in the same way as mixed border areas or inner-city interfaces. Members of the security forces often moved there for its relative safety.

David experienced 'a baptism of the Holy Spirit' in the late 1960s. This is a personal encounter with God, often involving physical or emotional healing. Bangor West started a healing service, which met after its Sunday evening service. Those who attended began praying for the safety of people in the security forces. 'People would give the names of policemen, and at the end of each session, the final thing we would do, would be to name those policemen. Many of them we would not know. The name would be given by somebody who would have cared for them.'

David shared two experiences which he believes demonstrated God's answers to their prayers.

A policeman was coming home one night, parking his car in his garage. As he walked to his front door he heard a voice saying, 'Run for it!' Which he did. The door was normally locked. This night it wasn't locked. He rushed through it and a hail of bullets came in after him. He's still alive. The other was a young man just starting off as a policeman. There was a bomb scare. He was on the beat with a senior policeman. The older policeman said to the young man, 'You and I will go down and warn people.' As he was walking, he heard a voice say, 'Fall flat!' Which

he did. And the bomb went off. He was covered with
shrapnel and when he was pulled out, he said, 'Who
called for me to fall flat?' Nobody had.

'If they think you are on a personal crusade,
they won't go with you.'

Husband and wife Stanley and Valerie Stewart ministered
in Clones, Co. Monaghan at the time of writing. Stanley
was ordained in 1997, after a career in teaching. He also
served as a part-time RUC reservist. He attended the special
General Assembly in 1990 which produced the Coleraine
Declaration on peace. The Coleraine Declaration
reflected the Stewarts' perspective even before Stanley's
ordination. He said, 'I can remember thinking, "God is
speaking."' Valerie was also a teacher. Both were involved
with faith-based cross-community initiatives where they
taught in Dungiven, Co. Londonderry, a town with a
strong republican movement. Because of the security risk,
Stanley wore concealed body armour and 'carried a side
arm as I taught in a secondary school'.

Stanley's first congregation was in Donagheady, Co.
Tyrone. They secured European Union peace funding to
renovate a derelict cottage in the grounds of the church
into a cross-community centre. They felt supported by the
congregation, but some people in the community – from
both nationalist and unionist persuasions – resisted their
work. They had been at university in Coleraine during
the David Armstrong controversy and the lesson they
learned was that if you wanted to bring people along,
it was important to move slowly and build trust. Stanley
said, 'If only David Armstrong had a support network. If
you run too far ahead it can be counter-productive. Yet

I have great admiration for his willingness to tackle the issues that weren't being tackled.' Valerie added, 'It's so important not to go out on your own. You must have others that you can trust, those people you can call who you know will pray for you. You have to gain people's confidence. If they think you are on a personal crusade, they won't go with you.'

CHAPTER 3

Victims

People who were bereaved or injured – or in some cases, both – *had no choice but to respond to the Troubles.* They have been forced to consider a range of responses: anger, revenge, hatred, bitterness, mercy, forgiveness, reconciliation and grace.

Victims' voices are often absent from public conversations about dealing with the past, so we do not understand how they suffered at the time, how they manage their pain, and how they live with the legacy of the Troubles. For these reasons, we spoke to more victims than any other category of people. Some said they didn't consider themselves victims; others called themselves survivors.

We have presented victims' stories holistically, but there are common themes throughout. Ministers and other members of congregations supported most victims after the incident. But some victims felt abandoned by their church. Others doubted God, some asked Him 'Why?', some lost their faith altogether for a time. Many were comforted by prayer and reading the Bible, or by the idea that a just God would judge the perpetrators someday. Bereaved children were inspired by their grieving parent or parents – usually mothers – who made sure they grew up without bitterness. Others found solace in memorials to their loved ones, such as plaques in their local church; and by hearing their names recited on Remembrance Sunday. They still needed pastoral care, especially on the anniversaries of incidents. Some received this care; others did not. We did not ask victims directly about forgiveness. Most of them brought it up themselves. There was a range of perspectives: some had forgiven the perpetrators, others had not, and some hoped they would forgive them eventually. We asked victims about reconciliation, and their views diverged widely. Some thought reconciliation was impossible and even inappropriate if perpetrators did not repent; others thought it should be central to their lives and the mission of the Church.

For most, their faith and the support of their ministers and congregations had helped them heal – or at the very least, cope. But very few had much to say about the wider Presbyterian Church in Ireland (PCI). It did not impinge on their everyday lives, and they had never heard of its peacemaking programmes. Only one person mentioned participating in such a programme, which he found helpful. Others attended special events for victims organised by PCI, but criticised them for being insensitive and lacking follow-up.

'It would be nice to have reconciliation, but at the same time our lives have been ruined.'

Anne's father lost his legs in a car bomb. He had retired early from the Ulster Defence Regiment (UDR), but was targeted because of his previous work in the security forces. Anne's mother developed dementia. Anne and her husband George cared for Anne's parents until they died. Anne said, 'We had a young family and our lives were wrecked.'

In those days, it was rare for someone to lose their legs and survive. But her father pulled through and learned to navigate life in his wheelchair. Anne's mother, who died before her father, was more difficult to care for. 'I literally lost my mother. It was quite horrific with her. I think a lot of it played on her mind, trying to deal with it.' Her father lived nearby in his own house until he died at age ninety-three. He was resourceful, always fixing things and even gluing down objects around his house, like lamps, to keep from knocking them over as he went about in his wheelchair.' She said, 'He was a very determined man, and that's how he survived. But we've missed out on our family growing up because they've had to grow up with Granda coming first.'

Anne's father did not speak about the incident. He suffered severe bouts of pain and was confined to bed. At times, the pain was so much he rang Anne to come and sit with him during the night. Otherwise, he tried to get out of the house every day. He attended church until the pain became too much. George said, 'He was more forgiving about it than I would be. He never spoke much about it. It was his way of coping.' This reminded George of his father, who found the body of his own nephew, a policeman, who had been shot. 'He never talked much about it either, although it affected him.'

Anne and George were supported by ministers in their congregations over the years, but they never expected or received counselling from any quarter. Their current minister is sensitive towards victims. They believe in the power of prayer. George was amazed that on the Sunday when his policeman cousin was still missing in another part of Northern Ireland, the Moderator visited his church and prayed that his body would be found. 'The Moderator didn't know there was a relative in the church. I got a phone call that afternoon to say his body had been found. I always felt he was speaking to me.'

Anne and George were frank in their assessments of the prospects for reconciliation. Anne said, 'It would be nice to have reconciliation, but at the same time our lives have been ruined.' George said 'it's not exactly anger' that he feels, but 'resentment that a lot of those boys who were at the back of those bombings are now in the government'. He is content to 'live with' people of the same religion as those who hurt his family, but thinks that 'Corrymeela and those places where they talk about reconciliation are contrived. It doesn't change the mind-set of your extremists'. Although George commended the churches for trying to promote reconciliation, he said their efforts would not get far because 'your extremists wouldn't be stepping through the church or chapel doors too much'. Anne was even less optimistic: 'You're talking about a lot of people that have been suffering and I don't think any church, or any chapel, can make a difference.'

'For me to reconcile with the boys that planted that bomb – there's no chance.'

Johnston served in the police before the Troubles started. He was among those sent to Londonderry to deal with the first outbreaks of serious violence in the late 1960s. Later, he was one of the first on the scene after a bomb attack. He extinguished the flames on a young girl, saving her life.

Johnston and Paula were not surprised when their daughter, Samantha, followed her father into the police. Their lives were shattered when Samantha was killed in a bomb attack. Paula said, 'To tell you the truth, we're not over it yet. I lay in bed for a long time, I must admit. They had me on some sort of tablet.' Paula has been especially haunted by the manner of her daughter's death. Her body was not intact to prepare for burial. Paula initially lost her faith. 'I didn't believe God would let such a thing happen.'

Their minister visited and provided support. The local Catholic priest visited Johnston and Paula the day after Samantha died, and later read a eulogy for her in his chapel. Johnston said, 'I worked with some very good fellas who are Roman Catholics. They stood here and cried when Samantha was killed.' Paula said, 'Gradually we started going back to church – but it took a while.' She found comfort in the Bible. 'I gradually came to the conclusion that it was meant to be, that there was nothing anybody could have done to stop it. My thinking was: Samantha's death will be avenged.'

Johnston and Paula remain active in the community – serving others helped them deal with their loss. When asked about reconciliation, Paula said, 'For me to reconcile with the boys that planted that bomb – there's no chance. The way that word reconciliation is used – it's meant to make victims reconcile with terrorists. I would not want to reconcile with Samantha's killers, or meet them. I would rather remember Samantha's face, not theirs.'

'I just leave it up to the day of judgement.'

Jane's son, Alan, was a policeman. He was murdered on duty when he was just twenty-five years old. 'The police sent out a welfare man after he was murdered. We laughed at the stupid questions he asked: "How do you feel on Remembrance Sunday?" Sure, every day is Remembrance Day. People who haven't come through it don't know what it's like.'

Jane feels Alan's loss just as much now, perhaps even more. 'On Father's Day in church, you see his friends there with their families. You see the children riding down the road with their daddies in the tractors. That hurts. We have lost the next generation. Nothing was ever the same from when he died. You go through life, but there's not the same joy in it.'

The minister, elders and others from Jane's congregation and community visited regularly. 'People called with us for ages and ages after. Our Catholic neighbours, too. There is more of a bond in the country, so there is.'

There is a memorial for Alan in her church. 'That will be there when we're all gone.' There is another memorial in the location where he died. 'The Catholic priest was there when they dedicated it.' The minister who was the Moderator when Alan died has stayed in touch, which means a lot. 'It's been some twenty-five years but he came up on a Sunday to our church not so terribly long ago and he visited the grave and took a photograph of the headstone.'

Each year on Remembrance Day, there's a wreath laid at Alan's memorial in the church. During the service, the congregation sings, 'Be Still My Soul, the Lord is on Thy Side'. In the years after Alan's death, Jane got through by praying and thinking about the words of that hymn. 'At night, when things were dark and you would have liked to cry, you thought: Lord, be still my soul. Before you came to the end of it, you would have calmed down.'

No one was ever arrested for Alan's murder. Jane has no desire to learn the identity of his killer.

> Alan's gone and me knowing who killed him isn't going to ease the burden in any way. I wouldn't like to be there when he's meeting his maker. I wouldn't want to be with him on his deathbed, either. He'll think about it, for everybody has a conscience. Through my faith I know there will be a day of judgement and he'll have to answer for it. For him to truly repent I think he would have to come here first of all, and meet whoever belongs to Alan.

Jane blamed the Rev. Ian Paisley for stirring up the hatred that led to her son's death.

> If Paisley had been more Christian, I don't think Alan would be dead today. I think the Troubles would have gotten nowhere and there wouldn't have been so many lives lost. And then when he got to the top, he sat down with a murderer. Whereas the likes of Gerry Fitt – he was a good man – but he wouldn't have given him the time of day.

Jane's late husband wanted to know who murdered their son. 'Maybe my faith was stronger. I just leave it up to the day of judgement.'

'You can't go forward referring to the past.'

Alice and her 12-year-old son John were injured when a bomb exploded. They were hospitalised for weeks and John had a leg amputated. 'The Troubles never bothered me that much until we were thrown into the middle of it all.' After the blast, Alice couldn't move, and she didn't know what had happened to John. 'I was lying in the street very badly injured. I couldn't be moved. I was just left lying there till help arrived. I was coming in and out of consciousness. I kept thinking: why is nobody coming to help me?' When she got to hospital, 'I asked about John and everybody would have assured me he was fine. But he wasn't.'

Two days after the incident, Alice's minister came to her hospital bedside to tell her that her son had lost his leg. 'It was good that my minister was there to break the news. My husband was in a bad state. He wasn't able to deal with it all.' John was moved to a bed beside his mother. 'I don't know if it was a good thing or not, for I had to witness a lot of his pain. Whenever he needed a doctor, he cried and cried. It took quite a while for somebody to come sometimes.'

John endured some complications from his surgery and fresh bouts of pain. Alice was thankful that her son came to view his situation positively. 'He wasn't positive to start off with, but he became positive. That was what saved me: the fact that he didn't complain. He never once said, "Why did this have to happen to me?"'

Alice's minister continued to visit. 'I prayed a lot that everything would work out all right in the end. But apart from that, what can you do? The only people that could help us at the time were the medical people. It was up to them to put us back together again.' Support came from other sources. Her husband was involved in rugby, and teams and fans from all over the island sent John souvenirs and notes of encouragement. 'We found out that there was a lot more kindness than evilness after the bomb. On both sides. People were very kind. They would always ask how John was. I knew the support was there and I could have got more involved in church activities if I'd wanted, but I didn't want to.' John and her other sons no longer attend church. 'Sure, that's how it goes.'

John is enjoying a successful career. Neither mother nor son are defined by what happened to them. 'I wasn't full of hatred for those who had done it, for I couldn't care less about them. I'd like to see justice, but it's not going to be done in this life.' For her, 'Reconciliation is the only way. Most families in Northern Ireland have been touched in some way by the Troubles. You can't go forward referring to the past.'

'It was prayer that brought me back to life again.'

Lisa's husband was murdered and she was seriously injured in the same incident. 'It was a horrifying night. I remember everything that happened. I was never unconscious.' Lisa was in hospital for many weeks and was confined to a wheelchair for five years. She has had 174 operations and still endures physical complications. 'It has been very hard now, it has, because I had three of a family to bring up. Two of them were still at school.'

Lisa was in hospital when her husband was buried, so she couldn't attend the funeral. Her minister and clergy from other denominations visited regularly. 'At one stage, round my bed there was six people between ministers and priests, praying at the one time. There was always some ministers or priests at my bedside every day. They were very, very faithful to me. That's what brought me here where I am now, the ministers and priests.' Lisa believes, 'It was prayer that brought me back to life again.'

On her husband's first anniversary, her minister
offered to conduct another service for him.
'Presbyterians wouldn't normally do a service for the
first year. There was a very big turnout. I thought it was
very nice of the minister offering to do that.' Confined
to her wheelchair and in considerable pain, Lisa didn't
attend church for about five years. 'But my neighbours
were all very good. The minister was very attentive. The
Church of Ireland, the Presbyterian, and the priests
– they never left me.' Lisa also received counselling
through a community organisation. 'But I still do have
nightmares and still waken up thinking about it and
all the rest. It'll never leave. But life has to go on for
your family's sake.' The members of her congregation
'rallied around me; they helped me all they could. I
can't say anything wrong about them because I would
be telling a lie if I did.'

Despite ongoing struggles, Lisa isn't bitter or angry.

I don't hold any grudges, because no parent brings
up a son or a daughter to go out and do the like of
that. I wouldn't meet them [those responsible for the
incident], I wouldn't face them but I wouldn't go out
looking for trouble. I know what I went through and
I wouldn't want anybody else going through it.

*'I didn't know there were boys and girls who didn't have
all this going on in their lives.'*

Jennifer grew up near the border and her father and
grandfather were in the security forces. Her grandfather
was killed when she was seven. 'We also lost lots of friends
of the family.' A year after her grandfather died, the Irish

Republican Army (IRA) ambushed the car when her father was driving Jennifer and her brother to school.

As bullets rained into the car, Jennifer's brother jumped out and hid behind a hedge. He was not hit. Jennifer followed, but a bullet lodged in the back of her head. Jennifer's father was not hit, so when the IRA sped away, he gathered the children in the car and drove back to the house. Jennifer remembers the blood, and how her parents held her on their knees as they waited for the ambulance. 'They said the Lord's Prayer, and I remember that as clear as day. It always stayed with me that prayer was the response. When I got out of hospital, I went back to school and nobody made a big deal of it. Life just went on.'

When Jennifer was a child, she thought everyone lived with such danger. One day at the kitchen table, her parents remarked that they were living through 'terrible times'. Jennifer responded: 'If Adam and Eve hadn't have done that.' She explains: 'I thought the violence was because of sin in the world, and this was how it was manifesting itself. I didn't know there were boys and girls who didn't have all this going on in their lives.'

Jennifer's minister visited the family after traumatic events and the congregation prayed for her family. She did not receive special counselling at church or from social services, nor did she expect it. The routine of her family's Christian life brought comfort. They had to vary their route to church each Sunday to avoid attacks, but they remained dedicated to their congregation.

Jennifer believes her mother carried a heavier load than she did, because she lost her father and friends, and her daughter was seriously injured. The day of the ambush, her mother heard it happen. 'She didn't know if her whole family had been wiped out.' A Presbyterian deaconess who ministered in the Royal Hospital helped her mother deal with her grief. 'I have not got a bitter bone in my body, and that's down to the parenting I received. She's not bitter now, but she still hurts a deep, deep hurt.' Jennifer also learned from her parents that coping with pain is not something that happens once and for all. 'It's a continual process of handing those feelings over to God.'

'If you haven't your neighbour, you've got nobody.'

John has been part of the same Presbyterian congregation in the Republic since his birth. 'We were very conscious of the Troubles here all along the border. At night you would hear explosions going off; you could hear gunfire. But you never thought it would come to you, until it did.'

After an incident affecting his family, their minister was kind, but they didn't receive a lot of support from the church, a congregation of just a handful of families. 'They were all quite scared, all quite withdrawn because they thought it was the start of a trend of going round all the Protestants in the area. One fella said to me: "You're alright, you've it over you now. Who of us is going to be next?" But lucky enough it didn't develop that way.' Fear prevented Protestants and Catholics from getting together more often. 'They could have had more mixed gatherings, but there was a lot of fear in the area.' At the same time, 'There was never any problem with carrying out your religion here in the south – contrary to what you'd be led to believe.'

John did not doubt God, but he asked why this had happened. 'I never got an answer to that question. But when I'm praying at night, I will still say prayers for as many Catholics as I would Protestants that are having problems with health and so on. The religion end of it doesn't matter to me that way.'

He laments that, 'There was a lot of hatred put into people at that time through the Rev. Ian Paisley.' He hopes people can come to see that they need each other. 'Reconciliation is living together. If you haven't your neighbour, you've got nobody.'

'I just prayed most of the night.'

John suffered severe injuries from a bomb planted under his car. His mother and wife Janet were standing in the drive as he backed it out of the garage, and witnessed the entire event. John never served in the security forces, so he could only conclude that the attack was a case of mistaken identity. 'I always worked with Catholic people. You couldn't take any bitterness towards them.'

Janet recalled, 'He thought he was going to die and he said, "Lord, I commit my spirit into your hands."' The couple had no phone so Janet rushed to a neighbour to ring the ambulance.

John spent twelve weeks in hospital. The pain was such that he does not remember much from that time. He has had eighteen surgeries and continues to deal with pain and complications from his injuries. 'We are thankful. There's many a one that has ended up in a wheelchair.'

Their minister came to the hospital and accompanied Janet home that evening. The congregation held a special prayer service the following Sunday. It was an era before trauma counselling became common. They fell back on prayer to get them through. John found comfort praying while he was in hospital, and after he returned home and was confined to bed.

Janet experienced heart palpitations after the event, and became anxious that they would be attacked again. 'I couldn't sleep so I just prayed most of the night, off and on. It was actually a really good time because you were so close to God then that you felt you could have reached out and touched him.'

The words of the Lord's Prayer – 'forgive as you have been forgiven' – helped them come to terms with what happened. Janet said, 'If you don't forgive, how are you to be forgiven? Hatred only wrecks you.' John was comforted by the idea that 'God would finally judge' those who had hurt him and others. 'If anybody repents, there's forgiveness of sin. If they don't repent, there's judgement. I hope and pray that they repent.'

'I hope if they ever asked the family for forgiveness,
we would find it in our hearts to do it.'

Robert's uncle, a reserve policeman, was shot dead by the IRA. His mother never got over her brother's murder. She was called to identify his body, and broke down at his funeral. One of her other brothers died early, which she believed was a result of the stress of the murder. 'She was probably quite bitter afterwards. There was a big impact on us as a family. It still very much rumbles through the family. It's always in the background.' Robert's uncle had been involved in cross-community policing initiatives. People from all backgrounds attended his funeral. 'He was taken in cold blood. We'll never know if justice will ever be seen for that act of violence. It's ingrained in the family: that he was murdered, rather than died. The gravestone says he was assassinated.'

The family received good pastoral support from their minister immediately after the murder, and in the years following. Later, when the family moved and attended another Presbyterian church, a pastoral worker whom his mother called 'the lady minister' visited regularly and encouraged her. Robert depends on the 'spiritual disciplines' of reading his Bible, praying, and receiving support from other Christians. 'I don't think there's any hope outside the forgiveness that Christ can offer. That has been what sustains me and sees me through. It doesn't matter who you are – that is what is required. We are all the same. I need his forgiveness and that is the way I have dealt with it.' At the same time, Robert finds it difficult when he is reminded of the murder – when something about the Troubles comes on the news, or he visits the family's cemetery plot. 'There are moments like the anniversary, or when I go up to mum's grave, because I go past my uncle's grave to get to it. I always think about the day – my mum shaking – she was emotionally distraught.'

Robert said there's 'been consistent teaching' in the congregations he's attended, but 'it's not Troubles-related. It's more about us and God and the fact that we all fall short and need his forgiveness.' In 1985, twenty-four Presbyterian ministers signed a letter that appeared in the *Belfast Telegraph*. Titled 'For God and His Glory Alone', it critiqued the way Protestant churches had responded to the Troubles and suggested that they should repent for their own part in them. This letter would inspire the formation of the trans-denominational group Evangelical Contribution on Northern Ireland (ECONI). Robert's minister signed the letter. 'I remember my mother getting really wound up over this. I said, "No, he's entitled to his opinion. We may not agree with him, but he hasn't said anything that's wrong.'"

The Lord's Prayer has shaped Robert's thinking, through reciting 'forgive us our debts as we forgive those who are debtors against us'. He believes God will judge those who have done evil: 'Justice is his, and not mine.' He is not sure how he would react if his uncle's killers asked for forgiveness: 'I hope they can make peace with their God, which means they will have to recognise that what they did was wrong, and ask for forgiveness. I hope if they ever did that and asked the family for forgiveness, we would find it in our hearts to do it.'

'I don't know if I've ever said: "I forgive them."'

Emily was four years old when her father, a policeman, was shot dead by the IRA. She was with her brother in an upstairs bedroom when the police came to inform the family. She opened the child-proof stair gate to let them upstairs. 'But other than that, I have no other memories of it at all. Which is maybe a coping mechanism – although I'm not sure many four year olds remember an awful lot.'

Emily recalls just one other incident from the time. A Catholic priest, who had prayed with her father as he lay wounded on the street, visited the family to offer his condolences. While he was there, they received word that Rev. Ian Paisley was on his way. 'There was a whole big ruckus to try and get the priest out before Ian Paisley was in! Can you imagine? People saying, "We need to get him out of here!" Why did it matter? It's not Ian Paisley's house!'

At the time, the family attended a Church of Ireland congregation. Emily believes it was her mother's faith that saw the family through. 'Mum released a statement saying she didn't bear a grudge. Maybe she didn't use the words "I forgive", but my dad would have wanted her to forgive whoever was involved. Her attitude determined how we responded too. I can honestly say I never once felt bitter.'

When she was a teenager, Emily's family began attending a Presbyterian congregation. She had become involved in its youth fellowship through friends at school. This congregation was supportive in practical matters like providing lifts for the children to attend activities, which helped her mother. 'Mum was probably the one who was least willing to leave the Church of Ireland because she and my dad had gone to that church, and there is a banner in our old church that was donated by the police in commemoration of his death.' Friends in the Church of Ireland had also supported her mother, praying with her, making dinners, and providing other practical assistance.

Emily did not talk much about her loss growing up. She did not want others to regard her as a victim. When the family moved to the Presbyterian congregation, the minister was aware of her father's death and very respectful. She was nourished by conversations with the minister, which covered a range of matters of faith and practice: he did not approve of women's ordination; she told him that she was considering becoming a Presbyterian minister. At university, Emily studied history, but she kept quiet in class. 'I wouldn't have talked to anybody in my history class about it because I didn't know who they were. Particularly in Irish history class when it was obvious that people were not like you.'

Emily is not sure if she forgives her father's killers. 'I don't know if I've ever said: "I forgive them." I think if they came to my door and asked me, I would say, "Yes."

But I don't think I would use the word now. I'm not bitter and I don't hold a grudge but that's very different from forgiveness.'

'I really prayed that [my father's killer] would seek forgiveness.'

Catherine's parents were killed in separate incidents during the Troubles. She was just six years old when her father was murdered in a bomb explosion. 'That bomb ripped everything apart. It affected every area of your life: education, family, everything. Mum struggled, and a bottle helped her get through it.' Catherine's mother had been left with four young children. Twelve years later, after her mother had recovered from alcohol dependence, she was killed when trying to defend Catherine's sister from an attack. Catherine's family were not churchgoers. Catherine became a Christian when her husband became born again and started attending a Presbyterian church. 'I think for the first time when I became a Christian, I started to understand things. There was a big void and God filled it.' While Catherine is convinced God helps her cope daily with her losses, she still feels the pain.

Because I'm older I'm thinking more of the loss now. My children missed out on grandparents. But I'm not bitter. That's because I have my faith. I love that wee verse: 'Trust in the Lord with all thine heart, and lean not on your own understanding.' That would be my rock. I think if I hadn't God, I'd go crazy because you've been robbed of so much.

The man who killed Catherine's father had been in the news around the time of our interview, which had re-traumatised Catherine and her family. 'You still have the physical reaction of fear and anxiety when you are reminded of the event. My sisters are very, very angry, whereas I prayed to God to take my anger away. If the killer came into this room now, I would love to ask, "Why did you do it?" But I have no hatred.' Catherine has even begun to feel compassion for the killer. This happened one day in church, as she listened to her minister pray. His prayer brought the killer to mind, and she thought: 'Forgive him. I really prayed that he would seek forgiveness and I really meant it from the bottom of my heart.'

Catherine never expected nor received specialist counselling. Ministers in the two Presbyterian congregations she had attended did not preach about the Troubles, although they prayed about them. She had no awareness of the wider denomination until a few years ago. 'To be honest I didn't know who PCI was until recently. Seriously. Because they've had no part in my life. It depends on the minister if they want to involve PCI, if they use their material or not.' She thought the churches now had an opportunity to help people heal, describing a comforting victims' service she had recently attended in a Church of Ireland parish. 'There's still a lot of hurt and anger. If I hadn't my faith, I might be one of the bitter ones.'

'There's no God. I'm not going back to church.'

Sarah's son, a policeman, was murdered on patrol. He was married with two young children. 'I just missed him so much. His wife never married again so we've kept close. We see his family nearly every day. He missed his daughter getting married. He has a wee granddaughter which he never seen.'

At first, Sarah was 'ready to give up'. She thought, 'There's no God. I'm not going back to church. But then I got over that and I got back into church.' The people who rallied around her helped her find faith again. Sarah's minister visited nearly every day. 'He was here all the time.' Many people from her congregation encouraged her.

Sarah lived in a primarily Protestant town so before her son's death, she hadn't thought about the Troubles much. No one else from her congregation was killed as a result of the Troubles. People in her congregation talked about events during the Troubles. But then they would 'forget about it'. Sarah couldn't think of anything specific her congregation or the PCI had done to address the Troubles. 'They don't engage with society or politics.' She didn't see how the church could contribute to current debates about the past.

But she finds comfort in her congregation's Remembrance Sunday service. 'They read out the names of all the ones that were killed in war, and then my son's name as well. There's always a wreath laid by his children at the cenotaph.'

Sarah thinks that Protestants and Catholics are more divided now than they were before the Troubles. She cannot imagine reconciliation without politicians showing leadership. 'They need to stop all this arguing and try to come to agreement, rather than fighting each other all the time.'

'Why would the man above take him?'

Ed and his father served in the police. One night, Ed was wakened by two colleagues. 'It was hard for them to tell me. But I made it easy for them. I says: "Is he dead?" The wee sergeant, he says: "He is." My stomach sank. Then I left because I knew mummy was on her own.' Ed's mother, Laura, had already received the news.

They both questioned God. Laura recalled a visit from one of her husband's colleagues. She kept asking him, 'Why would the man above take him? He was a good man. He must have stayed till two in the morning listening to these questions. I couldn't accept it.' Their minister and elders visited. Ed said, 'The reverend was very good – he visited us a dose of times. I always questioned him. Why does the man above let this happen?' Ed's minister replied with, 'The usual stuff – the Lord has a plan, the good fruits picked first – he was trying his best. I felt sorry for him because he couldn't give me any answers. And to be honest with you, I wasn't taking it on board.'

Despite their doubts, Laura and Ed continued to go to church. Over the years, Laura found comfort reading the Bible. 'The Lord will help you and keep you going, although it's still hard. Being a Christian is what has kept me going.' Ed prayed and read the Bible. 'I wasn't getting the answers I wanted. But I still go to church – you can't blame the church.' He saw 'a lot of bad things in the police, but I didn't become an atheist'. Ed won't take communion. 'I live by the values of the Presbyterian Church and I believe in Christ, but for some reason, I can't take that step. I have questions about it all, especially after daddy's death.' Ed is angry, but not bitter, that the men he believes killed his father are 'still walking about free'. Even so, 'I didn't go out and try and shoot them. Once you cross that line, you're morally wrong.'

Their family is prayed for in church at the time of the anniversary. There are memorial plaques in the church and the Orange hall. Ed said, 'It's nice to look at during church. At least he's remembered. On Remembrance Day, there's a wreath put on that plaque. That helps, but it doesn't replace the man himself.'

Recently, their congregation has become involved in inter-church initiatives. Some local Catholics attended a cross-community meal at their church, including the mother of a republican paramilitary. 'The current minister is probably not aware – he hasn't lived here long enough to realise who she is. But this young fella targeted daddy and now his mother's sitting in our church. It's alright reaching out but how far do you take that?' His mother responded, 'I was sitting beside the lady. The man above says you have to reach out. In a sense you do forgive. You're a Christian – you have to.'

'I've my own way of dealing with it, which is accepting that was God's plan.'

From childhood, the Troubles were a way of life for Stephanie. 'I couldn't even start to name how many people we knew had been shot or blown up.' Her father was a UDR reservist. 'We children knew we weren't allowed to answer the door.' When she was a teenager, a bomb exploded under her father's car as he left for work. Stephanie was woken by her mother shouting, 'Your dad's dead!' They did not have a telephone, so Stephanie and her sister ran in their pyjamas to a neighbour. As they passed the burning vehicle, she heard her father calling out, 'Don't leave me!' He survived. The family was determined life would go on. 'I had done the first part of my O-level Maths on the Monday. The bomb went off on the Tuesday, and I went back to school on the Wednesday and did the second part – and passed it!'

Sixteen years later her brother Jason was murdered in a bomb attack. 'My brother was not involved in anything. He was out doing an honest day's work. And that's why he died – because he was a Protestant.' Jason was the only son. 'All daddy's farm land was to go to him. Daddy never really got over it.' When Stephanie walked away from the graveside after the funeral, she was overwhelmed by panic.

The minister and congregation rallied around the family. 'The minister brought a lot of comfort. He would say a wee prayer. I was hanging on every word. Mummy would've phoned the minister at all hours of the day and night, just when things became very unbearable.' Stephanie's mother later worked in a cross-community group, where 'she was a voice for forgiveness. It was her firm view that if she came face to face with the person who detonated the bomb, that she would forgive, because that is what God would want her to do.' Stephanie was inspired by her mother and her own faith grew. 'I've my own way of dealing with it, which is accepting that was God's plan. I know it wasn't His act, but I haven't questioned God as to why He allowed that to happen.'

No one was arrested for the bombing. 'Would I like to know who detonated the bomb? Not really. It's not going to bring me any comfort. I know there will be a judgement day for that person. I believe if that person was to reach out to God and ask for forgiveness, well, God would forgive him.'

On Remembrance Sunday, her brother is named in her childhood church. But she now attends a large urban congregation, and feels her pain has been forgotten.

'Because we've had the peace process, I'm not sure how focused the church still is on helping victims. The focus has moved away from families who have been victims. Some Presbyterian ministers might not understand because they didn't experience the Troubles like we did. But it's still important that they are able to get into that zone of sympathising with the family.'

Stephanie is frustrated by politics. 'The politicians don't really care about people who've lost their loved ones. My brother died at age twenty-four for nothing – for absolutely nothing! The Good Friday Agreement hasn't changed anything. We're in the same position, fighting about who should be running the country.'

'When you were praying, it was like you were talking
to your best friend.'

Ruth has lived with the Troubles for as long as she can remember. As a child, she wasn't allowed to play with her doll's cot because her father, a prison officer, used it to hide his personal weapon so he could access it quickly in case of attack. Her husband, a policeman, was murdered on duty. She was left with three young children. 'I couldn't believe it. I kept saying, "Will he be okay?" I don't know how many times they had to say to me, "He's dead."'

Ruth told her children their father was in heaven. When her 4-year-old daughter prayed at night, she asked God to make her father 'come alive again like Lazarus'. Ruth said, 'It was heart-breaking hearing that, as well as dealing with your own grief.' A few days later, a Catholic was murdered in retaliation. 'I was interviewed on TV, and I said, "My husband wouldn't have wanted this. He was about life, and love, and getting on with people."'

Ruth later found out who killed her husband but forgot his name.

> I forgot because I didn't want to remember it. I didn't want to know the name, because I didn't want to hate anybody. If I met the person who killed him, I don't know if I could forgive him. I have no hatred. I think so many people have hatred, which they need to get over, because we're all God's people. But I was almost angry at God for letting him die.

Ruth went to the Church of Ireland at the time. She joined a Presbyterian congregation a few years later because it offered more children's activities. There is a memorial plaque for her husband in her mother-in-law's Church of Ireland parish; and a memorial banner for him in the Church of Ireland parish she attended. Once they joined the Presbyterian congregation, the minister provided pastoral care, and her husband is mentioned on Remembrance Sunday.

Ruth got through by 'almost constant' prayer. 'I prayed when I was out in the car, when I was peeling the potatoes, when I was cleaning the house.' She had studied the Bible daily before her husband's death, but after the incident 'my concentration was gone' and she found it difficult to read. 'When you were praying, it was like you were talking to your best friend. Maybe you didn't get an answer straight away, but you knew that somebody was listening.'

Ruth still questions God. 'Sometimes even now I would say, "Why did you let that happen?"' These questions came back when her daughter married, and her son walked his sister up the aisle.

That wasn't his job. But then, at least we had him. You
have to look at your blessings. I think that God just
eradicated that anger through His love. If I had have
had my way, I wouldn't have got up every morning.
But there was always a force behind me, making life
acceptable again. You look at your children, and you
think, 'Look at them. They need me.'

> *'Reconciliation doesn't mean you have to*
> *give up your faith.'*

Ross grew up near the border. He recited a list of young,
only sons – the traditional inheritors of farmlands – who
had been murdered by the IRA. His school headmaster,
a part-time UDR man, was abducted, tortured and
murdered by the IRA. His brother Mark was injured in
a bomb. Ross remembers seeing him in hospital. 'He was
just – unrecognisable.' Traumatised, Ross went home and
'prayed earnestly that he would live'. Mark survived, but
had many physical complications. 'Dad never really came
to terms with it. He was in bits – the oldest boy in the
house.' His father died of a heart attack a few years later.

Ross's family were Church of Ireland. Looking
back, he believes that while he learned 'good morals',
the 'Gospel wasn't preached there'. He also attended
Presbyterian youth clubs. 'I was searching for God after
the bomb, but I didn't know where to find him.' He was
born again in his early twenties after attending Brethren
Gospel meetings. Ross soon joined an Elim Pentecostal
congregation.

Mark pursued his passion, art, and was successful in
this profession. He developed epilepsy, which he managed
with medication.

Mark hadn't found Christ at that stage. He would push the barriers. He would go to a tent mission and light a pipe and sit and smoke. And say: 'You can't put me out, I'm here to hear the Gospel.' But he was searching too, unknown to the rest of us. His art was starting to depict what it felt like to be a victim. He was out there finding victims, getting people's stories.

Twelve years after the incident, Mark died due to complications from his epilepsy. 'My mum never got over it. She took his watch and she wore that for the rest of her life. She wouldn't talk about it. Her first son. Gone. She lamented that till the day she died.'

Ross was heartened to learn that Mark had become a Christian. 'He wasn't your conventional Christian. He visited prisoners in the H-block. He wasn't going to church with a shirt and tie on – he was trying to think outside the box. If you're a believer in Christ, you extend the hand, however hard it might be. If you don't, you're going to end up with the same mind-set as those that afflicted these atrocities. My brother tried to do that through his art.' Ross also finds solace in God's justice. 'There mightn't be justice here and now, but in the long term, justice will be done. A sovereign God has all things in the palm of His hands. That makes it liveable – to a point.'

Ross moved to the Republic twenty-five years ago and joined a Presbyterian congregation. He felt that Presbyterians in the Republic 'kept their heads down', but they were 'not downtrodden – not like the older generation after partition'. He met Presbyterians who were republicans, and 'they're born again and as much a Christian as northern unionist Christians. The northern

Presbyterian would like to think they were beat to pieces down here, but we're not. We are accepted.' He believes northern Protestants often think that 'reconciliation means compromise', but for him 'reconciliation doesn't mean you have to give up your faith'.

'In Christ, we have something that is able to change the human heart.'

Seven-year-old Michael Davidson was being driven home from Sunday School by his uncle. As they approached his house, Michael noticed many cars parked outside. A plain-clothes policeman approached. 'Are you Michael?' The man led him inside, where his mother was weeping. 'A lady I didn't know came over to me and said, "Michael, you're going to have to be very brave. Your dad's been in an accident."'

Michael's father, a police officer, had been shot. After three weeks in hospital, he was taken off life support. Michael was at his grandparents' house when his mother brought him the news: 'Your daddy's gone to heaven.' Michael was sent to stay with friends for two weeks and did not attend the funeral. 'I came home, and it was all done. It wasn't talked about. But those events are imprinted on my mind like it took place yesterday.'

Michael attended a Baptist church and his mother had a strong faith.

My mum was prepared to forgive those who murdered my dad. Nobody was ever caught or convicted. She never instilled any bitterness or hatred towards the other community or the IRA. I am very thankful I was brought up in that environment because I know that other people who experienced what I did ended up going down a very different path.

Michael felt the pain of his father's absence at key events in his life, like graduating from university, marriage and having children. He remembered his mother sometimes 'struggled', but her faith helped her through. On Remembrance Sunday, she could never make it through the service; she would become upset and leave. His grandfather used alcohol to cope.

A year after his father's death, Michael became a Christian. The words 'Your daddy's gone to heaven' had been playing on his mind, making him aware that 'if I died I wouldn't go to heaven because I hadn't made that commitment to Jesus that my father had'. One night at bedtime, he told his mother he wanted to become a Christian. He knelt by his bed and 'said a simple prayer'. Michael believes God used his father's death to bring him to faith.

As a teenager, Michael attended youth clubs with his friends in a Presbyterian church. By the time he left secondary school, he felt called to become a Presbyterian minister. 'As a Presbyterian, I believe absolutely in the sovereignty of God, and I believe that God knew the plans he had for me. What I'm doing now is a direct consequence of my father's death.'

Michael's experience helps him understand those who have suffered due to the Troubles.

Because we have so many folks in our denomination who have suffered personally, and so many who have been denied justice, there's often a feeling that certain peace initiatives are a betrayal of folks who have died and suffered. But the word of God speaks very powerfully into our context in terms of Jesus saying, 'Love your enemies. Pray for those who persecute you.' In terms of forgiveness, we struggle. I would have been criticised for things I said from the pulpit where I was encouraging people to put that into practice.

Yet he remains hopeful: 'In Christ, we have something that is able to change the human heart, to take away bitterness and sectarianism.'

'Forgiveness is a decision.'

Aaron never met his father. A policeman, he was murdered by the IRA while Aaron's mother was expecting. 'That incident framed the rest of our lives, but we didn't let it define us.' His mother ensured her children 'didn't harbour hatred'. They prayed together daily. 'She's still a big prayer warrior for the family and she continues to be involved in praying for peace and reconciliation.'

Aaron became a Christian at a young age and attended youth activities at his church. The Troubles weren't mentioned much among the congregation or from the pulpit, but the congregation supported them. 'Church was a safe space where we established lifelong friendships. It offered an alternative to being out drinking in the town or fighting with Catholics, which was the choice of some of my friends from school.' He remembers wanting to join the police or army. 'Looking back, I was probably having thoughts of revenge; that if I joined up, I would be able to get these people who killed my father. I imagined what that would be like, and what it would feel like. But that was before I had come into a full thought process of what reconciliation looked like.'

Aaron began to think more critically about his faith when he attended Queen's University. During that time, he participated in PCI's Preparing Youth for Peace programme. 'I still have the big blue folder with all the different things from Preparing Youth for Peace. It got me thinking – this is what Jesus meant when he talked about forgiving your enemies.' He was influenced by Rev. Steve Stockman, who was then Queen's Presbyterian chaplain. Steve organised a student trip to South Africa to meet people who had been involved in its peace process and to volunteer in a township. Other Christian mentors and friends, some of whom also lost their fathers, supported Aaron, especially when he felt 'lonely' and needed to talk.

For Aaron, reconciliation involves forgiveness, and a willingness to balance the tensions between justice and reconciliation. 'The ultimate injustice is Christ dying on the cross for stuff He didn't do. When you look at the world through that lens, you look at things quite differently.' News reports about the Troubles can trigger old hurts. 'I can't speak for others, but for me, forgiveness is a decision. It's not a decision you make once. You have to make that decision again, and again.'

Aaron thinks PCI is split between those who want justice at the expense of reconciliation, and those who want to respond in what he sees as a Christ-like way – by showing mercy. 'I don't feel like the church led from the front in terms of responding to the Troubles and I don't think they are leading now.'

Aaron doesn't advocate a South African-style Truth and Reconciliation Commission but he thinks there should be 'some forum or some form of public outworking of reconciliation, that acts as a vehicle to inspire people to move forward'. He wants PCI to contribute to debates about what this could look like. 'Somebody needs to have some vision and take some leadership on how to deal with the past, because it's not going away, is it?'

'Some in the Presbyterian Church are more interested in the ones that pulled the trigger than the ones that got the bullet.'

Henry and Jane are life-long Presbyterians from congregations near the border. Some years before they married, Henry was injured in a sectarian attack. Jane's first husband, a businessman, was murdered around the same time. Henry said, 'You were just going from one incident to the next and it left life very cheap. You were depending on your faith in God and your family around you to keep you going. There was no outside help from anybody.' There was a handful of small Presbyterian congregations in their area, all of which were without a minister. He said, 'That left Presbyterians in this part of the country isolated and forgot about.' When asked why no Presbyterian ministers wanted to come, Jane said simply, 'They were afraid. There were too many murders in the area.'

Jane's first husband was abducted before he was murdered. She and her mother-in-law spent two anxious nights in the home of their neighbours, who were Catholic. Around midnight on the second night, she was wakened by Rev. Samuel Roberts (a pseudonym), the minister in charge of the vacant congregations. 'He took me downstairs. The police were there to let me know a body had been found. There was a doctor there – I got

an injection, and Samuel Roberts took me back upstairs.
Next morning, Samuel Roberts was there to waken me.'
After the funeral, Jane continued attending her own
congregation, which had a minister. 'But that minister
never came to visit me or spoke to me about the murder.
I was at church every Sunday. I suppose he seen me at
church and thought, "Oh she's alright, she's moving on."'
Jane continued to teach Sunday School, 'but I never went
back to the choir, because in the choir you had to face the
people in the pews. I wouldn't have been happy facing
people, the way I was.'

Even though Jane wasn't part of his congregation,
Samuel provided her with pastoral care. She ran her late
husband's business until she married Henry, and Samuel
stopped by and visited her and her mother-in-law there.
'We couldn't talk about it because we were so upset. His
mother would have sat by the fire and cried. But Samuel
Roberts would have called in and it gave us a lift. At least
he was thinking about us.'

Few ministers were willing to come to the area to
take communion services. Communion is infrequent in
Presbyterianism, with some congregations having as few
as two services per year. One minister who was willing to
conduct these services would not drive any closer than six
miles from their church. Henry said, 'Was his car more
important than our car was a question we asked ourselves
many a time!' On one occasion, Henry was driving the
minister and they were stopped at an IRA checkpoint.
When the minister later told Henry they should report
it to the police, Henry said: 'If you report it, you need to
keep your diary free next week because you'll be up here
doing a few funerals. They know who I am, so I would
advise you to think again.'

Though disappointed by a lack of care from PCI, Henry and Jane are still seeking pastoral support from it. They mentioned three different Presbyterian initiatives for victims they had attended. Two of the events left them feeling more wounded than healed. In the mid-2000s, a Moderator and two other ministers visited their presbytery and invited victims from the surrounding area to come and tell their stories. Henry described it:

> There were the three of them and maybe twelve or fifteen of us. After a prayer and a reading, they said, 'Tell me your story.' We had never spoke out in public about it before which was a bit rough. They called it a 'fact-finding mission'. They promised they would do interviews in other places, and when it was over, they would come back to us with a report on what PCI intended to do to give comfort or support to victims. We're still waiting.

PCI held a special service for victims at its headquarters in Belfast in 2009. During our interview, they produced the order of service from the event. Henry said, 'There was no more care in that than in a blooming cattle mart. I was going to take Jane out of it, it was that bad. We were so upset.' For them, the title of the service, 'Remembering and Healing', and the hymns sung, implied they should be 'over it'. Afterwards, during tea and biscuits, Henry said, 'The four men who took part in that service never walked round to speak to anybody there.'

The couple also had the order of service for a local event organised a few years ago, on behalf of the Moderator. It was choreographed by a minister in a nearby congregation, a man they believe sympathises with and understands victims. Jane contrasted the services:

> That evening in Church House really opened the wounds instead of helping. The other service was more helpful. I met the Moderator after the service and he invited me to sit down and talk with him. The next day he rang, and he wanted to see the place where Henry was injured. He did seem to take more of an interest in what was going on.

But Henry and Jane felt many local ministers didn't support the service. There are more than twenty congregations in the presbytery, and all were expected to be involved. Henry said,

> Some ministers did not announce it to their congregations. One minister held a session meeting on that night. Another one didn't announce it but attended a meeting in the local high school – it was more important. Sometimes I think they just want us to go into a corner and lie down and die. The sooner we disappear, the better for some.

It also hurts when they see PCI encouraging dialogue with republicans, because they feel victims have been abandoned and ignored. Henry said, 'Those ministers that are pushing hard for reconciliation, I don't think have a true understanding of how people like us feel. We are no way as close with our Catholic neighbours here as we were forty years ago. But those ministers – they brush you off. Some in the Presbyterian Church are more interested in the ones that pulled the trigger than the ones that got the bullet.'

'A lot of people would like a visit from their minister,
but maybe he doesn't remember.'

Edna and her young daughter had just returned home from the shop, where they had bought potatoes. Edna told her daughter, 'By the time your dad is showered, we'll have tea ready.' Her husband worked in an army barracks nearby. She heard an explosion. 'I said, "Oh my God, they've killed our men."' Edna's anxious wait went on for hours. Neighbours called in, but they didn't have any news. Around 10.30 pm, the police and the Presbyterian minister arrived. 'As soon as I saw them come in, I knew that it was final.'

Edna turned to alcohol to deal with the pain.

I took a sleeping tablet and half a glass of whiskey every night going to bed. I remember one night thinking, 'If this child takes sick, how on earth are you going to take her to a doctor?' Something stopped me in the middle of the stairs, and I went down and threw it into the sink and that was it. There was Somebody guiding me.

Edna didn't always want to go to church. But her minister visited, and a neighbour from her congregation encouraged her to keep going. Enda also read a devotional booklet called *Our Daily Bread*. 'I would have read that in the morning and then a wee text of the Bible. That gave me great comfort.' Her daughter received a stipend from the Presbyterian Orphan Society until she turned eighteen. 'I wasn't working at the time so was on very low income. That's something I will always appreciate.'

Edna's GP encouraged her to seek counselling. The wait on the NHS was long, so she contacted a victims' group. The group's outreach worker counselled her and her daughter. Enda now works for the group. She encounters grieving Catholic families. 'I was living in a bubble and I was a bigot. Now I see that our tears are exactly the same.'

Enda has not forgiven her husband's killers. 'When I'm saying the Lord's Prayer, I never say: "Forgive us our trespasses, as we forgive those who trespassed against us." I discussed that recently with a Church of Ireland minister and he said he had several in his congregation that does exactly the same thing.'

The minister who was in her church at the time of her husband's death has left, and Edna feels that her new minister does not understand her experience. As years passed, it seemed people forgot her loss. 'People thought I was fine. But that's wrong. It was a struggle and sometimes it still is a struggle.'

In the mid-2000s, Edna attended an event organised by the local presbytery, where the Moderator met victims and listened to their stories. This was the same process mentioned by Henry and Jane, but in a different location. 'We met for an hour or two. That was it, end of story, book closed. They wanted to know what they could do. But it didn't go anywhere.'

As the anniversary approaches each year, Edna's struggle increases. In her work, she has found that others have the same experience. 'Whether it's been five years, twenty-five years, thirty years – a lot of people would like a visit from their minister. But maybe he doesn't remember.

Just a half hour – that would mean a lot to us. Have a wee prayer and the support.' Edna realises that ministers who are new to congregations may not have that local knowledge, but thinks PCI should remember its victims and keep its ministers and elders informed about their pastoral needs.

'He said, "There's no God to let a tragedy like that happen."'

Judy's husband Ben lost his parents and another relative in a single incident. Judy and Ben had two young children and Judy was pregnant. 'You always came over as being very strong,' said Deborah, Ben's sister. Judy replied, 'I had to be strong, for the children. Ben was not the husband I had married. Even the boys would say, "Daddy used to play with us, and daddy didn't after that."'

Although they lived in different towns, Judy and Deborah supported each other. Judy's minister was always available. 'If I was worried about Ben, I'd only to lift the phone and he was at my door. If I'd rung him in the middle of the night, he would have come to Ben. The organist in the church, she was very supportive. But the rest of the congregation didn't know what to say to us.'

Sometimes Ben left the house in the middle of the night. They feared he would harm himself. Deborah and her husband accompanied Judy's minister to look for Ben on those nights. 'We would find him in the graveyard, sitting on the grave. We saw the red tip of the cigarette – he was sitting on the graves, smoking. I didn't go in the graveyard, but my husband went in with the minister. It was so sad.'

Judy was raised in the Church of Ireland but attended Ben's Presbyterian congregation after they married. She didn't become a Christian until after the incident, through attending mission meetings. 'I needed somebody to help me get through those days and that's why I came to the mission. My parents prayed with me and they helped a lot with the children. I needed God – I really did need somebody to cling on to. Through prayer – any worries that I had, I just put to Him.'

Ben's faith was shattered. Judy explained, 'He said, "There's no God to let a tragedy like that happen." Thankfully, before he died, he did return to God. He always would have talked to our minister but he even said to him, "There's no God to let the likes of that happen", which was understandable.'

Deborah, raised Presbyterian like her brother, later joined the Church of Ireland. She thought her Presbyterian congregation could have been more supportive. 'Maybe we didn't ask for it. Or maybe it appeared we didn't need it as much. It was friends and family rather than the church that helped.' Not long after the incident, some of her family left the Presbyterian Church for Rev. Ian Paisley's Free Presbyterian Church. While Deborah was not entirely sure, she thought it was in part because the Presbyterian Church was perceived as not responding well to the Troubles. Her local Church of Ireland minister offered her more encouragement. 'I always remember the Church of Ireland minister saying, "Every year when the daffodils come out, that's when you remember them."'

Both said victims need ongoing support from their churches, even years later. Judy said, 'Around the anniversary, it would be nice to see something from the church to say, "We were thinking of you." The minister, someone from the Presbyterian Woman's Association – to say, "We're saying a wee prayer."'

On the 25th anniversary, Judy asked her minister if the incident could be marked with a service. 'He said the service for that Sunday was all prepared. He didn't change the service, he just added it on.' Deborah said, 'He could have changed it to make it meaningful.' Judy added, 'It wasn't an appropriate memorial service. He did let us take part, but we asked. Maybe the church should have said, "Do you want to hold a wee memorial service?"'

On a more recent anniversary, the local Orange lodge dedicated a memorial plaque. Family, friends and local clergy attended. Judy said, 'Even the priest was there.' Deborah added, 'The priest was the first one there and he was sitting under the picture of the queen!' Judy said, 'It was nice they didn't forget about them. But then that was the Orange.'

Neither could think of anything the wider PCI had done to respond to the Troubles. Deborah once attended an inter-church meeting for victims. It wasn't helpful. 'The speaker was preaching at me about reconciliation, and I was the one who had suffered. I obviously would have given reconciliation quite a lot of thought. I didn't need him coming telling me what I ought to be doing. People don't understand. They have their own agenda.'

CHAPTER 4

Security Forces

Some Presbyterians responded to the Troubles by joining the security forces. They perceived Northern Ireland as under attack by terrorists and believed that by joining the security forces they could help restore normalcy to society. A few said the Troubles did not motivate them to join: they were simply attracted to the security forces as a career, their family had a history of service, or it was 'just a job'.

We spoke to men and women who chose to work full-time and part-time in the Royal Ulster Constabulary (RUC), which became the Police Service of Northern Ireland (PSNI) in 2001; the Ulster Defence Regiment (UDR), an infantry regiment of the British Army that existed between 1970 and 1992; and the Ulster Special Constabulary, more commonly known as the B-Specials, a reserve force that existed between 1920 and 1970. We also spoke to men who had joined the RUC before the Troubles. We interviewed wives of officers to gain a fuller perspective on how their husbands' careers impacted family life.

Every person we spoke with had family members or colleagues killed during the Troubles; some were injured themselves. They coped by praying, reading the Bible, and receiving support from their ministers and congregations. Some questioned God. Others were angry but insisted their faith kept them from taking the law into their own hands and seeking revenge. Many felt the Presbyterian Church in Ireland (PCI), and other churches, did not fully understand and support victims and those who worked in the security forces. They were deeply concerned that republicans were 're-writing history', and unjustifiably portraying the security forces as villains.

'On the second day down at the hospital,
my mother dropped dead at my bedside.'

'On the second day down at the hospital, my mother dropped dead at my bedside. She was forty-eight years of age.' Samuel Malcolmson, a police officer, was seriously injured in an Irish Republican Army (IRA) gun attack. He knows who shot him, but he was never prosecuted. 'I've often wanted to say to him: "When you shot us, did you feel any remorse when you realised my mum dropped dead at my bedside, or did you feel great? I got two for the price of one."' Samuel was in hospital for a year and his family's minister brought his father to visit. 'But ministers since then, they think, "I don't need to do anything."' His wife Gayus recalled: 'I went to church on Sundays and I took the children to church. But I can honestly say that the minister, nobody from the church ever asked how we coped, or offered help.' Samuel added: 'At the same time, some congregations in the Presbyterian Church did stand by us, and helped us financially.'

Samuel continued,

This is a problem I have with church: ministers will come and, if you forgive [the perpetrator], you nearly get a clap on the back: 'Good, you've moved on.' I have moved on, but no way will I ever forgive. If he wants forgiveness, let him come and ask me. There's no forgiveness in me, but it doesn't stop me from moving on.

Samuel could not work again because of his injuries. He joined a group for wounded police. Some churches have hosted this group for special services or talks. He recalled speaking in one church and explaining how members of the security forces were 'living a lie' by instructing their children to conceal their parents' occupations.

> The minister in that particular congregation interrupted me. He said: 'You need to explain more.' I just happened to look round and five or six people stood up and there were two or three police officers, a prison officer and a UDR man. I looked round at the Rev. indicating that these people maybe want to say something. Each of those people said: 'He is right, we're living a lie.' That minister apologised to me and said: 'Sorry, I'm out of touch.' He didn't even realise members of his own congregation had to live a lie and security force people are still living that lie.

Gayus recalled that while there were prayers in their congregation for people who were injured, 'There was never any in-depth consideration of why things were happening.' She had questions that have not been answered. 'How do bad things happen if God has a plan? There was no explanation from a minister or anybody as to why [atrocities] were allowed to happen. I believe in Christian beliefs and Christian ideals, but I couldn't honestly say I believe God has a plan.'

Samuel and Gayus thought PCI had been 'silent' about victims. They were hurt when Rev. David Latimer from First Derry Presbyterian publicly befriended Sinn Féin's Martin McGuinness, speaking at a Sinn Féin Ard Fheis (party conference) in 2011 and at McGuinness' funeral in 2017. McGuinness had been a member of the IRA in Londonderry. Samuel said, 'You don't win any support among victims by getting up there and saying Martin McGuinness was a saint, or words to that effect. If Latimer realised just how damaging that performance on television was to victims, I think he would hang his head in shame. Those that gave their lives and suffered were the real peacemakers.'

'I wasn't a combatant, I was a police officer.'

David joined the RUC when he was eighteen and served thirty-four years, ending his career in the PSNI. Other members of his family served in the security forces. His father was shot dead as he returned home after UDR training. 'I remember every minute of what happened. I remember going to identify him and half his head blown off. It's something you don't forget. I am aware of the people who did it, members of the PIRA [Provisional IRA], and I believe I know the person who ordered it be done.'

His father's killers were never prosecuted. 'When you look at some of these politicians, and I know that some of them where involved in terrorism – it's difficult. You hear people now talking on the news, saying the RUC were part of the problem. I didn't join to be part of the problem, I joined because I wanted to serve the community.' His wife Violet added, 'Your worry is that when the history of this is all written, the RUC will be put in the same bracket as the paramilitaries, the terrorists.' David agreed. 'I wasn't a combatant, I was a police officer.'

David's mother was a widow for thirty-one years and from the day her husband was murdered, she never spoke his name. A decade after his death, David and Violet took out their wedding album to look at with his mother, hoping that the photographs of her husband in it would encourage her to talk about him. Violet said,

> It came to a photo with him in it and she just turned the page. No comment. It came to the group photograph at the end of the album, and she started pointing to this one and that one and saying something about them. She pointed to some and said they had died. David pointed to his dad and said, 'Mum, what about that man there?' She just turned to David and looked him straight in the eye and said, 'It's a long time since I've seen him.' That was it. She never, ever mentioned it again. That was heart-breaking.

David was initially angry about his father's murder, but this subsided after a few months. Violet said, 'We were taught the difference between right and wrong. You knew in your heart of hearts, going out and looking for revenge was not the Christian way to do things. We were taught to turn the other cheek.'

Unlike many police families, David and Violet told their children what their father's job was and said not to conceal it from their friends. Violet said, 'We always thought what if, God forbid, anything happened to David when he was out on duty and then I had told them that daddy was a postman for example. I was going to have to

turn round and tell them I'd been lying all along.' David
worked long hours, but Violet received support from their
congregation and other police wives.

> That support did help, but it was still scary. One
> Christmas Eve, I had to do Santa Claus because he was
> out working. I can remember me sitting looking at
> the hands of the clock and praying: 'Lord, just let us
> get to Christmas Day with nothing happening.' And
> watching the hands go from twelve into Christmas
> morning and thanking God that we'd got to Christmas
> and nothing had happened. I did have my faith to
> call on. But prayers weren't always answered.

David and Violet thought that some in PCI did not fully
understand the experiences of victims and those who
worked in the security forces. Violet believed that during
the Troubles, Presbyterian leaders in the Republic should
have pressured their government to pursue paramilitaries
who had fled across the border. David recalled attending
a function and speaking with a former Moderator. 'He
found out my father was killed. He asked me about a
particular member of Sinn Féin and I told him what I
thought. He whispered in my ear and said, "You're too
close to it." I thought, "Isn't that an awful thing to say?"
He wanted me to forget about this man's past.' Violet
added, 'That person had not experienced what David had
experienced. I think if he had experienced it, he wouldn't
have said that.'

They were also upset by what Rev. David Latimer
said at Martin McGuinness' funeral. David said, 'It was
just like a knife going through my heart when I heard
the Rev. Latimer describe Martin McGuinness as near to

a saint. It really was, to the point that I could have left the church at that stage. I phoned Church House [PCI headquarters] about that because I thought it was an awful, awful statement.' Violet agreed, 'We were hoping Church House would say something [in response to Latimer] but that never really did come.'

David reflected,

It might be easier for people to reconcile who weren't directly involved. Whenever people talk about reconciliation, I think about the people that were killed on the border because they were supposedly touts. I remember going and lifting their bodies and seeing cigarette burns on their faces and a hole in their head. How do you reconcile with people who do that? I've no issue with reconciliation. But it'll be reconciliation without forgetting what happened.

'Reconciliation? Maybe in the future,
but I don't think so at present.'

Gwen shook her head. 'You see that statue with the fingers reaching from one side to the other?', she asked, referencing the *Hands across the Divide* sculpture in the city of Londonderry, where she lived as a child. 'There will never be peace in Londonderry or in this country because the Catholic people won't let it be so.' Gwen had Catholic friends when she was growing up, people who lived in the same street. 'They just abandoned me. They didn't want to know any Protestant people. I found that quite hard to understand: friends one minute, against you the next. You didn't know who to trust or speak to.'

Gwen's husband was in the security forces. Not long after the family moved to a rural area, 'Unionists Out' was written on the handrail outside their home. 'I'm a Protestant. I didn't say I was a Unionist. How could these people know how I voted? They just took it for granted.' The front door was pelted with eggs; burning objects were thrown into the yard. Church brought some sense of routine and normalcy. 'Apart from going to church, we just prayed. What else could be done? It was my job to keep the children safe and protect them. I was a member of the local Presbyterian church and probably watched by so-called neighbours as this was a mixed area.' She doesn't remember any ministers ever preaching about the Troubles. 'Who gave what was happening that name – it was a terrorist campaign. Maybe not talking was their way of dealing with it. I think it was very odd that nobody offered any help or guidance. If there was, I didn't hear about it.'

Gwen's parents moved from Londonderry, too. 'Their home was continually under attack from people from a Catholic housing estate, not far away. It had become unbearable to live there.'

The praise Martin McGuinness received at his funeral rankled with Gwen. She showed us a magazine article she had saved, lauding McGuinness.

The article made me very, very angry because of all the people that had been murdered and hadn't a chance to defend themselves. McGuinness was a terrorist. It was total evil what these people did. McGuinness felt no remorse for anybody. He had one object, a united Ireland. Reconciliation is not a helpful word as the hatred Catholics have shown to Protestants will take a very long time, if ever, to be put to one side. My parents or the Presbyterian Church never taught us to hate anyone, only the opposite. There is one God, how you worship him is up to each individual. Maybe we could have respect and tolerance for each other's way of worship. Reconciliation? Maybe in the future, but I don't think so at present.

'When we're talking about what did the church do to reconcile, people feel it did nothing.'

Rodney Beacom and two of his RUC colleagues were transporting a prisoner when their car was ambushed. 'When you are in a life and death situation – and you could die – sometimes people turn to God. That's what I did.' Rodney was not a Christian then. 'I cried to God, "Help me." I firmly believe he saved my life. Not only did he physically save all of us, but there was a sense of his presence.'

Growing up in Fermanagh's rural borderlands, Rodney was confirmed in the Church of Ireland. As a teenager, 'I found reasons not to go to church.' As a policeman, he accompanied his Presbyterian wife to church on his one weekend off each month. When he returned from hospital and couldn't yet go back to work, 'Sundays were free – I no longer had the excuse!' Rodney was discharged from the police on medical grounds two years after the attack and took up other employment. He struggled with anger and thoughts of revenge. 'All those emotions you go through – there's always a consequence for those close to you. The daddy that went out that morning to work wasn't the daddy who came home after he got out of hospital.'

People from his congregation visited and prayed for them, and they received a lot of support from their GP. His wife made tea and played hostess, even though she was struggling as well. 'There was nobody else to do it. You were left to get on with it.'

Although Rodney had experienced God's presence during the attack, he didn't become a Christian right away. 'Years passed before I had what the Bible calls "the peace of God that surpasses all understanding". It was eleven years from the terrorist incident until I had a relationship with Jesus.' Within two years, Rodney was an elder; two years after that, he was training for ministry. He now ministers in four congregations near where he grew up: Lisbellaw, Lisnaskea, Maguiresbridge and Newtownbutler.

Rodney's first memory of church is the funeral of his father's cousin in Lisbellaw Presbyterian. She was the first female member of the security forces to be killed in the Troubles. 'There at the front was the coffin, draped in the union flag. I was seven years of age, and I remember my father getting down on his knees and crying.' Rodney now pastors members of the woman's family, and many other victims. He identifies with them through his own experiences. 'Theological college can't prepare somebody to go and sit with those people.'

Rodney attended an inter-denominational prayer service for IRA victims on the same day as Martin McGuinness' funeral. At the service they expressed sympathy for McGuinness' family, but many victims were disappointed by what Rev. David Latimer said at the funeral. They had also hoped that PCI would issue a statement around the time of McGuinness' death, acknowledging victims' pain. 'There are victims saying to me, "What has the church done for me?" When we're talking about what did the church do to reconcile, people feel it did nothing.'

He added,

> I think there should be acknowledgement that the church didn't do what it could have done. A public apology that we weren't what we should have been – to say we didn't get it right all the time. There should be acknowledgement that there is hurt on both sides. So, there should also be a public apology to society, because we all contributed in one way or another to what happened and didn't happen.

'The churches should be speaking for victims.'

Drew Harris was serving as Deputy Chief Constable of the PSNI at the time of our interview; he became the Garda Commissioner in September 2018. He joined the police when he was eighteen, following his father into the RUC. The rhythms of police life have shaped him since boyhood. 'I wouldn't have seen much of my father, seven days a week. On Sunday morning he would drop you off at Sunday School and he went straight back again to the station.'

The demands of shift work made it difficult to attend church every week, but Drew felt his minister and his church understood and supported him. 'My minister had a strong sense of support for law and order, and how that related to other civic institutions which are important for a free society. His prayers of intercession always involved the security forces. While I couldn't always attend church, the minister would have often been in our house – a regular visitor.' Drew spoke of 'the obscene futility' of the Troubles – 'murder for murder's sake, year after year' –

and how important the minister's support and the care of his family had been.

Drew recalled that during some of the more difficult years of the Troubles, Moderators made regular visits to police stations. 'I remember being in a border station and the Moderator and his wife came along to see us. Had a cup of tea with us and brought a cake. It was just nice that somebody would come along and spend a bit of time with you and ask you how it was going, because it was a thankless task.'

Drew thought that level of support from PCI has become 'a bit lost' since the end of the Troubles; and that all the churches haven't quite grasped how they could contribute in the present period.

I think the debate about dealing with the past is a very legalistic one and victims should have a voice, and the churches should be speaking for victims. The Presbyterian Church buried an awful lot of victims and it's almost as if, in some ways, there's a bit of amnesia about that. The Troubles live on with us and the trauma and hurt from that has reverberated into other things, like drug abuse, alcohol abuse, domestic abuse, and a lot of people still in dire straits. There is a coincidence between those areas most deeply ravaged by the Troubles and where these issues are most prevalent. The churches aren't engaging enough around those issues.

'There's no way Christ, if he walked this earth, would say that.'

'Wait! Wait!' Beth heard a familiar voice shouting, and feet running down the corridor. She was prone on a hospital trolley, riddled with gunshot wounds. It was the minister from her church. A doctor yelled, 'We have no time to wait!' Her minister ran faster. 'He took my hand and prayed as they wheeled me into theatre. I don't remember anything after that for a long time.'

Beth's minister was listening to the radio when it was reported that a policewoman had been shot. Although Beth was not named, he knew it was her and rushed to hospital. Beth had always wanted to be a policewoman, but her parents convinced her to pursue another career. When the Troubles started, she and her husband Richard joined the part-time reserve.

Beth and Richard were driving to work when they were ambushed. It was the day before their daughter's first birthday. Richard was not hit. As the gunmen fled, a man from a nearby building site rushed to the scene. Richard was so upset that Beth, propped up in the workmen's passenger seat, had to give directions to the hospital. 'I was convinced I was going to die. I didn't even have to call on the presence of God. God's presence filled me with peace.'

As she recovered, Beth faced multiple surgeries. A doctor advised her she was likely to die young, and that she would not be able to have more children. She 'had a bit of a breakdown' and received psychiatric care. The words of a friend who was a minister in the Church of Ireland gave her hope. 'She used to say that verse in the Bible: "God will give you abundantly more than you ever asked."' Beth had another child and now has grandchildren.

Before the incident, Beth and Richard were involved in the Christian Police Association. 'We prayed for our colleagues and drew close to families after any incident.' A year after the attack, Beth's injuries prevented her from going back to her regular job, so she was medically discharged. She was devastated. A colleague from the Christian Police Association gave her a hymn book. 'He said, "On the days you can't read your Bible and you can hardly talk to God, I want you to promise me that you'll read one of the hymns and think about the words." That took me over many's a hump.'

Like Henry and Jane, whom we met in Chapter 3, Beth attended a regional victims' meeting in Newry organised by a Moderator in the mid-2000s and the service for victims at Church House in 2009. Unlike Henry and Jane, her experience was positive. 'There were people who had never been allowed to express how they felt and how they had been let down by the church, by society, by friends, by family. The Moderator was the most caring and divinely driven man. It meant a lot to the people who were there.' Beth also mentioned a Presbyterian minister in another part of Northern Ireland who organised a special service where injured police officers took part. A former officer with a brain injury who is usually unable to attend church did a reading. 'That was recognition.'

Beth empathises with her former police colleagues, believing that God can help them too. But many of the injured and bereaved 'have completely lost their faith because of what happened to them'. She thinks ministers who demand forgiveness push them away.

They talk about how we – the people who were shot and blew up – have to forgive these people. Any time my colleagues go to church they'll end up crushed by ministers because all they ever get is that they have to forgive the perpetrators. How can you say to a man who lost two legs and an arm: 'You have to forgive the people that did that to you'? That's obscene. There's no way Christ, if he walked this earth, would say that.

Beth experiences regular pain and sitting on hard church pews exacerbates it. She still hosts a home Bible study group, but attends church less. As the years pass, people in her congregation seem less able to understand. 'I pray all the time. Victims in general – not just injured police – feel forgotten. We were the peacemakers, and these terrorists that are in our government are holding us to ransom.' Beth said groups like the Wounded Police and Families Association are trying to raise awareness of the needs of police and victims. 'But I don't know where the Presbyterian Church have been.'

'When they passed me, they sneered and ... laughed.'

Craig grew up on a farm near the border. His mother's family were farmers in what is now the Republic. After partition, 'They became objects to be got rid of. My mother's father always felt that he had been wronged by the makers of this new State and his rights weren't protected.' Craig's father was in the B-Specials. 'I used to clean his gun for him, being the eldest in the house. It was almost as tall as me. When their weapons were inspected, his was always commended. This is what he told me, which was perhaps an incentive for me, because I was saving him a job.'

As a child, Craig watched as family friends were killed in the Troubles. He felt 'a great sense of injustice. In my mind, people who were brave enough to put on a uniform were going out against this force of evil.' He joined the RUC. Early in his career, a colleague was murdered by a car bomb. 'At the very impressionable age of twenty, I had the dubious job of carrying a comrade's coffin, hearing his two little daughters walking behind crying, "Daddy, daddy." I knew that more than half of their daddy's body mass was not in the coffin and that sand had been used to replicate the weight that wasn't there.'

A few years later, Craig was travelling in an armoured car that struck a landmine.

> Later I became aware of the names of the people who were alleged to have been involved in the attempted murder of myself and my colleague. They have never answered on earth for what they have done. But with my Christian belief, I know that unless they fully repent, there is a day of judgement coming. That is the only solace I can draw.

Craig knows the identities of others who murdered his colleagues but have not faced prosecution. In one incident, colleagues were killed and maimed for life. Years later, Craig was walking down the street in his hometown when he passed the men he believed were responsible. 'When they passed me, they sneered and looked me straight in the eyes and laughed. It was the defining moment in my life where I realised that there was no real justice in this world. Those men had been allowed to come back across the border without the fear of being lifted and put before a court.'

Craig also believes that some Catholics tried to save the lives of police. He described receiving anonymous phone calls that warned them not to travel on certain roads at certain times. 'On a human level, they were people who recognised we were not as bad as we were being portrayed. That helps me to be reassured that the milk of human kindness is within everyone.'

There were Troubles-related bereavements in his congregation. Craig thought his minister 'did an absolutely outstanding job, listening to people and making himself available. He conveyed the Biblical precepts by which we need to align ourselves.' For Craig, those Biblical precepts have translated into an openness to former enemies.

> Someone asked me not that many years ago, if the then Deputy First Minister [Martin McGuinness] were to extend the hand of welcome to me, would I be able to shake it? I had to think about that for some time, knowing a little more information on the inside about his activities than the ordinary average person in the street. That is a moral question that did cause me some doubt initially. But if Her Majesty the Queen can shake him by the hand, well I would be a very poor person if I couldn't do likewise.

'There's evil on both sides and we're here to stop the evil.'

James served part-time in the UDR for three decades. He worked as a repairman, completing jobs for people from all religious and political backgrounds. Over the years, he helped organise cross-community events in his area, including fundraisers for people in need.

James lived in a rural, border region. There was one village where people always came out to stone their patrol vehicles. One night, the priest was stopped during a routine vehicle check.

> I addressed him as Father, and I said to him: 'Your locals are stoning us and somebody is going to get

hurt some time. Can you not get that stopped? We're not here to insult them – we're here to guard them, to look after them. There's evil on both sides and we're here to stop the evil.' Then I thanked him. He couldn't believe that I talked to him as a human. Funny after that, the stones stopped so he must have said in his church, 'Stop it, them people's not as bad as we're making them out to be.'

James said in his area, Presbyterians joined the security forces in greater numbers than any other denomination. He believed this was a noble choice. 'I need my church and I think it was my prayers that helped me come through what I have seen. But if it came round again I would like to see the churches encourage people to join – to do the right thing.' He was disappointed by a Presbyterian minister who once said to him, 'There should be no such thing as walking about with a gun.' James said: 'I walked about with a gun for thirty years and never fired a round. Just because I picked up a gun, he thought I was a terrorist. But I wasn't a terrorist, I could see other ways out of it.'

'Our job was to keep the peace.'

'I was one of the last to move out.' Andrew was a police officer who married a Catholic before the Troubles. The violence had sparked major population shifts in cities, and it was no longer safe for a Protestant policeman to live in what was becoming a Catholic area.

Andrew and his wife attended their own churches. The children were raised Catholic. 'When the children were making their First Communion or their Confirmation I would have went. But then you realise that you are leaving yourself wide open. Because people were being attacked going to their churches; some people were killed outside their churches.'

Many of Andrew's friends and colleagues were killed. 'I've been to quite a few funerals, Protestants and Catholics. You've got to keep a faith and hope it doesn't happen to me. You feel a bit guilty – *why was it not me?*' He leaned on his wife for support. 'You came home at night and talked about what happened during the day and what you'd seen. But you tried not to let it affect your own personal private life and your own faith.'

For Andrew, the most difficult period was during the republican hunger strikes in 1980–1.

> I fell back on Bible verses. One was, 'Yea, I am always with you, even to the very ends of the earth.' Verses like that were going through your mind, especially during the hunger strikes ... Once, after a night's rioting was over, I realised that a nail bomb was just beside me, and it hadn't exploded. I thought, 'There but for the grace of God, you could be dead.' I remember going to police some of the hunger strikers' funerals, and the atmosphere was raw. For about eighteen months it was touch and go whether or not the country would descend into civil war.

Andrew drew some encouragement from sermons. 'I remember the minister preaching one day, "Put on the breastplate of God, the sword in one hand and the shield in the other." I also remember, "The Lord is my strength and salvation, my sure defence in times of trouble."' Andrew was clear that he was a defender: 'The police and military did not go on to the streets to kill people. The terrorists' idea was to kill, maim or seriously injure people from the Protestant or Catholic side in the tradition of sectarian warfare, or to kill soldiers or policemen. Our job was to keep the peace.'

'I never stopped praying – morning, noon and night.'

Donald, a police officer, grew up near the border before the Troubles. He remembers Sunday School excursions to Donegal. 'When the Troubles started that all fell on its face. I wouldn't have been across the border six times in all my working life.'

Donald's wife Susan tried her best to give their children a 'normal' upbringing. That wasn't easy in a house with bulletproof windows and elaborate alarm systems. The children watched their father check for explosives under the car before he drove them to school. Donald said, 'You couldn't hang [police uniform] shirts on clotheslines. They could identify your house with that.'

Susan said, 'Donald was away from early morning to late at night and we were trying to be a wee normal family – having their friends here and letting them go to all the different activities like sports and boys' and girls' brigade.' It was common for the phone to ring during the night, calling Donald to an incident. Susan said, 'We didn't realise it for years but when the phone would ring, and Donald would have to go out to another scene, our son would lie there awake till his dad came home again.'

Susan appreciated support she received from other officers' wives, and through children's activities at church. 'The church was there for us. I never stopped praying – morning, noon and night. Prayer for Donald's safety, and for all the families that were going through this terrible time. And that our children would be okay.'

Donald had a nagging sense that all the churches could have done more during the Troubles, but admitted it was difficult to think of specific actions they could have taken apart from condemning violence and pastoring the bereaved. He said, 'I'm not sure if there was very much anybody could do. I have always found that in most stressful situations all people want is a shoulder to cry on instead of you trying to do something for them.'

'The first day you're in the police, they tell you
how many of you will be dead within a year.'

'The first day you're in the police, they tell you how many of you will be dead within a year. They tell you that you're not allowed to go here, you're not allowed to go there. I was thinking: I'm only eighteen! Hold on a wee second. I can't believe how naïve I was.'

When Sharon joined the police, she had not grasped how putting on the uniform would make her a target. At that time, female officers were not allowed to carry firearms. 'You might get a phone call at midnight to say, "There's a threat out on policewomen so watch yourself." Then you had to go to bed. You've no gun, so if they came for you that was it – your time was up.'

Sharon coped with the deaths of many colleagues. A close relative was badly injured in a bomb attack on a civilian target. This also affected her. 'She just sat there in her wheelchair and cried and said she wished she was dead.' Sharon managed by focusing on aspects of her job she enjoyed and by praying. 'You nearly expected to die young because so many of your friends were going. So, you just used to pray. I remember many a time going up a laneway and praying: "Please God, don't let this be a set up. Let us be safe."'

Sharon also questioned God. 'Those people were good – why did God let these things happen? Where is God?' She never got fully satisfactory answers for her questions but believes, 'God wants the best for everybody. It's people who do the [bad] deeds. I just accepted it. There'll be bad times and good times – that's life.'

Sharon participates in Remembrance Day services for her colleagues. 'It's essential especially for the family and friends to let them know they haven't been forgotten. A lot of people were hurt when the police changed from the RUC to the PSNI because they felt, "Well, what was that all about?"' At the same time, Sharon looks forward. She has been part of an inter-church group for more than twenty years. 'People need to reconcile and get on with each other and live together as equals.'

'What we heard at church didn't do any harm.'

Bruce was a farmer and part-time reservist. Two brothers were full-time police. One was killed on duty. 'The danger was always there. It was your job and you had to accept it. You always thought it would happen to somebody else.'

Bruce was initially 'very angry'. But his anger turned to acceptance.' 'A good way to come to terms with anything is to be a busy person.' He lived in a mixed area and had attended a mixed school. Neighbours of all denominations came to express their sympathy. His brother had specialised in community policing in an interface area and had a good relationship with a local priest. The priest read at his brother's memorial service.

'A Free Presbyterian man wouldn't come to the service because of that. But we didn't see anything wrong with the priest doing a reading.'

While his family grieved, they were not bitter. 'We are glad that we did not act in any bitter way or seek revenge. I give praise to my parents for setting a good example. I'm sure what we heard at church didn't do any harm.'

Bruce was a Methodist at the time of the incident. As a child he had attended the Presbyterian Sunday School. Both the Methodist and Presbyterian ministers visited the family in their bereavement, and when the Methodist congregation closed some years later, Bruce joined the Presbyterians. 'When something terrible happened, all ministers would have prayed about it. They were always trying to keep people on the right direction. The churches' role was to try and keep people from getting hysterical and to carry on life as normal as possible. There is a limit to what the churches can do, and I don't think there was anything else they could have done but see that you were able to continue your life – that you weren't too depressed.'

'I was talking to God when it was happening and that saved my life.'

Joshua survived two IRA attacks while serving in the police. Two colleagues died in one; he was seriously injured in the other. 'I was [shot] and I was in a police car and I just remember saying, "How long does it take to die?"'

Joshua regarded this question as a prayer. 'I believe in God. I probably wouldn't be considered a "saved" Christian. But there were serious incidents when I was talking to God when it was happening and that saved my life.'

Joshua has been faithful to his congregation over the years, even though his police duties meant attendance could be sporadic. His comment that he wouldn't be regarded as 'saved' reflects a belief among some evangelicals that people must have a 'born-again' experience to be a Christian.

Joshua's minister visited him in hospital, and organised prayers for him in churches of all denominations. 'The prayers probably didn't do me any harm, helped me get through.' He didn't seek further support. 'My parents went to church and they were asked about me every week. If they had sensed I needed anything, the minister would have come to me. Support was there in the background if I needed it.'

Joshua attends a Remembrance Day service for his colleagues every year and sees this as an important way to mark their deaths. He wants to look to the future.

Reconciliation is probably the closest word we can get to describe what we want to do [as a society] because we are still in many areas so divided. I'm willing to talk to anybody about my experiences if it will help. I'd have difficulty talking to a terrorist who's still adamant that killing is a good thing to do. If someone was reasonable and indicated that what they engaged in was wrong, I would talk to them. But as far as our stories – and this will sound a bit brutal – who cares? Will anybody listen to us?

'I still subscribe to the Christian principle of forgiveness, however difficult that is at times.'

Peter joined the RUC in 1961, towards the end of the 1956 IRA campaign. All police stations, including numerous small country stations, were open to the public twenty-four hours a day. Peter recalled, 'To maintain that, the station duty officer was on from 9 am until 9 am the next day, but with the privilege of bringing his bedding down from midnight. His next duty was a three-hour patrol that same morning.' Officers living in the station paid for a cook, were responsible for polishing the floor and all other cleaning, and contributed to fuel and light.

When widespread rioting began in the late 1960s, police were ill-equipped to deal with the outbreak of violence.

> We were pulled all over the province – sometimes being left out on the streets overnight. Protection against stone throwing and petrol bombs was a waterproof coat, a motorcycle helmet, and a short baton. When street rioting was overtaken by another IRA campaign, later interspersed with other loyalist and republican terrorist groups, the police force became stronger and better equipped to meet the challenge.

Two of Peter's family, also police officers, were murdered by the IRA. Three of the twenty-five men who joined the RUC with him in 1961 were murdered. During an IRA ambush, a colleague sitting beside Peter was shot, but survived. Later that same week, Peter chanced upon the Ulster Defence Association (UDA) parking a car bomb outside a Catholic pub. 'I had an armed confrontation with the fleeing driver and next I was inside the blast zone trying to clear the area when the bomb exploded.' A passing motorist was killed.

Peter said, 'Morale within the RUC remained high despite the enormous risk and continuing anxiety of families. Comrades were assessed by attitude, ability and honest commitment; differing religions were of no significance. All were basically doing the same job while at the same time trying to protect one another.'

For Peter and others, the grief over the murder of loved ones was compounded by 'the establishment's response'. He recalled his younger brother, who was

a single lad aged twenty-three years, a choir member and youth leader in his church. The compensation paid to my parents just about covered the funeral expenses. That would have been the same for the parents of my brother's young constable friend who was also killed in that booby trap bomb. My mother's lament was, 'Is that all my lovely son was worth to them?' The enormous sums paid out to terrorists over the ensuing years have done nothing to lessen the hurt.

Peter said,

My family and the Presbyterian Church in Ireland taught me to respect all truth, to be honest, and to have respect for others. The church never spoke of politics but constantly prayed for government, for peace, and for the bereaved and injured. It is difficult to see how the church could have done more. Naturally when family members were murdered, the church shed tears too and offered the utmost support.

Neither Peter nor his family sought specific help, 'But we are forever thankful for the church's sympathy and caring.'

For Peter,

Young impressionable people can get caught up in bitter conflict based on biased conditioning, rumours and half-truths. Then there are the calculated, sadistic murderers who set out to ambush, booby trap and bomb men and women going about their daily business. Compounding all that is that very few of such people – numerous as they are – have ever been before a court of law or offered heartfelt sympathy. But I still subscribe to the Christian principle of forgiveness, however difficult that is at times.

'Them kind of things keep you very angry – people trying to blow you to bits.'

Neil served in the B-specials in a republican town. He was shot one night returning from work. Every man in his platoon was targeted over the years. 'I was the only one to be hit really bad. The rest of them, they had their windows blew in, bombs left under cars. Them kind of things keep you very angry – people trying to blow you to bits.'

Neil had some narrow escapes before his injury. His platoon was regularly attacked, out on patrol or in the barracks.

There were holes in the walls in the barracks, where they peppered the walls. They knew rightly there was guards on at night, and they tried to put a bullet through where they reckoned you were sitting. I always lay in an old bunk in the back of the room – let them shoot away. You had to get on with life. You couldn't bow down to them boys.

Neil was in hospital for six months. He was able to lead an active life for a few years, but his pain increased. Many more surgeries followed; some made him worse. 'But the doctor told me if the bullet had gone in half an inch either way, I never would have walked again. That was brave and close, so it was.'

Neil tried to return to church, but the pain of sitting on the hard pews left him 'so crippled I could hardly walk out again'. His ministers over the years have visited regularly, as well as a member of the congregation who is now in her nineties. Neil's wife was a faithful attender until she died. The congregation would not let him pay for the meal that was held in the church hall after her funeral. 'There must have been a couple of hundred in the hall. I tried for a month to pay them for the meal, but they wouldn't take any money off me. I thought very highly of the church after that.'

When asked how the wider church responded to the Troubles, Neil said, 'They didn't really respond at all. I wasn't asking for any response from anybody so nobody came. I just got on with life the best I could.' He is pessimistic about the future. 'Protestants couldn't walk up the street in this town now. People think the Troubles are over. They aren't over.' Pointing to his heart, Neil said, 'The Troubles are in here, as far as I can see.'

'We are in danger of history being re-written from a republican point of view.'

'It was a lovely sunny day.' Ray was a postman and part-time sergeant in the UDR. He knew the people on his route, which wound through a rural borderland.

Normally on a sunny day, the front door of this house would be lying open. But it was shut. I just put the letter through the letterbox and was turning away from it. One of the gunmen came out from behind a shed. The first bullet hit me in the chest. I was wearing my body armour and it stopped the bullet, but it spun me around. The second bullet missed the body armour and went through the right lung straight into the back.

Ray ran. The gunmen pursued. He had lost the use of his right hand, so he fired back with his left, hitting and wounding one of the gunmen. The gunmen ducked behind some hedges. Ray was not sure if they had fled, and he was still some way from his van. 'To stay where I was, was to die one way or another. They were either going to come back and whack me, or I was going to die with my lungs filling up with blood.' Ray reloaded his gun and made his way to his van. He drove to the police station and honked the horn. An officer came to the door. 'I've been shot!' The officer thought he was joking, but Ray shouted again. This time the officer got a car and took him to hospital.

Ray served sixteen more years, retiring not long before the Belfast Agreement was reached. Some situations he encountered were more traumatic than the attack on his life. He had to comfort the grieving family of a colleague he had recruited into the security forces. He attended a harrowing bomb scene. 'Whenever I saw the bodies of those young men and the others screaming with injuries – that was the worst night of my life. I didn't sleep for a week after that.' Ray voted against the Agreement because he was opposed to the release of prisoners. 'The things I have seen and the good friends that I've lost – why would we allow someone to walk about with a letter saying he's not wanted for anything? That's corrupt – I couldn't see any moral justification for it.'

Ray read his Bible and prayed, but he still questioned God. 'Sometimes it was hard to have faith when you saw what God allowed to happen. Why is God allowing somebody to do what they've done, and get away with it, and leave so much sorrow behind? I still haven't an answer.' He knew Presbyterians who joined the Free Presbyterians or the Baptists. 'I know very genuine people who felt their church was letting them down and there was something more for them in the Free Presbyterian Church. I didn't see anything wrong with the way the Presbyterian Church conducted itself. It wasn't the church's place to play politics; it was there to support its members.'

Ray wants churches to tell a fuller story about what happened during the Troubles. 'I think the churches should do this because we are in danger of history being re-written from a republican point of view. I have not seen remorse from those people. In fact, they are proud of what they did. I couldn't reconcile with those people. They went out to kill their neighbours. If lies continue to cover the truth, unless the truth is told time and time again, it will disappear.'

CHAPTER 5

Those Affected by Loyalist Paramilitarism

Some Presbyterians joined loyalist paramilitary organisations, or family members joined such groups. We spoke with three men who had belonged to such organisations; and one woman whose husband was imprisoned for paramilitary offences. Rev. John Hutchinson converted to Christianity in prison and became a Presbyterian minister. His own experience of forgiveness has convinced him that Christians in Northern Ireland should be asking hard questions, like 'What does it mean to love your enemy?' The other interviewees chose anonymity.

The secret nature of paramilitary organisations makes it impossible to know how many of those who joined also attended Presbyterian congregations or remained affiliated with the Presbyterian Church in Ireland (PCI). Some who joined had attended Sunday Schools or youth clubs and maintained a nominal affiliation with Presbyterianism. Others were motivated to join paramilitary organisations by leaders like Rev. Ian Paisley. Some rejected the church. Others were converted to Christianity while imprisoned.

It is a common belief within working-class loyalist communities that PCI, indeed most of the Protestant churches, stood on the side lines condemning paramilitarism and washed their hands of those who got involved. It is felt that PCI has not tried to understand why they made the choices they did. They contrast their own exclusion with that of republican ex-combatants, who they perceive as being welcomed by PCI and having their perspectives heard. Like those who served in the security forces (Chapter 4), they believe republicans are 're-writing history', and PCI is not challenging the republican narrative.

'What does it mean to love your enemy?'

John Hutchinson grew up in a Pentecostal church in Portadown. 'Both parents were Christians. I never heard any hate towards Catholics, or the Catholic Church.' At sixteen, 'I completely walked away from the church.' As the Troubles wore on, his brother joined the police. 'I thought, my brother's in the firing line here. Part of me resented the police for not doing more against what I would have seen as republicanism getting a free run because the authorities' hands were tied. That's what eventually led to me doing something myself about it.'

John joined the Ulster Volunteer Force (UVF). 'If somebody had told me at that point I would end up in prison for attempted murder, I'd have died laughing. But there were resentments building up, there was anger.'

John was captivated by the powerful bond that came with being part of a secret paramilitary organisation. Cutting himself off from family and old friends, and identifying with UVF comrades, 'made violence easier.

It almost made doing what you were doing seem right, although I would have to say I lived desperately against my conscience.'

When John was twenty-eight, he was arrested and spent six and a half years in prison. On his third night in prison, he remembered the Christian teachings of his youth. 'I knelt down and asked forgiveness for what I'd done.' John began to read his Bible and the works of Reformed authors like Charles Spurgeon. 'I became convinced of Reformed thinking. That led me to Presbyterianism.' Although he had been estranged from his wife, Glynis, for two years, she visited him in prison and he tried to convert her to Christianity. 'Glynis used to go out [from prison] and say, "He's telling me how bad I am, and he's sitting in there!"' John eventually stopped heavy-handed evangelising of Glynis. A year before he was released, she sought out an Elim Pentecostal pastor who led her to faith.

The first church service John attended after prison was at Hill Street Presbyterian in Lurgan.

> There was communion at the end of the service. I asked the wee man at the door, 'My wife and I are believers, would we be able to go to the Lord's Table?' He just put his arms around me and hugged me. That welcome he gave me, in about fifteen seconds, it spoke as much to me as the sermon did.

John flourished in Hill Street with the support of its congregation and the minister, Rev. Drew Moore.

> But I found it hard to shake off the whole paramilitary thing. I was very Free P[resbyterian]-orientated, in that I would have believed there was a just war going

on, and that as a Christian it was alright to defend yourself in a war situation. There was still a lot of anger, even hatred, and Drew Moore was a colossal help for me to shift that away.

John soon went for ordination. While training at Union College, he tried to conceal his past, avoiding conversations with other students about their backgrounds and previous experiences. 'One day the wee janitor came up to me. They had been giving out tickets for parking [infractions]. He said to me, "John, I was going to give you a ticket, only I knew that if I gave you a ticket, you could've blown my car up on me!" I said, "Dear me, this is out."'

John said that in general, he has been accepted in PCI, and as minister in the Leckpatrick, and Moy and Benurb congregations. But finding a ministerial placement was not straightforward. While seeking a congregation,

> I preached for a church [without a minister] and [I was later told that at the] congregational meeting to vote on who would be the minister, one woman stood up and said, 'No terrorist will ever stand in our pulpit!' I'm not naïve enough to think that people might not have a few question marks, but that got to me a wee bit.

Over time, John began to believe that his own presentation of the Bible to his congregation, while emphasising individuals' need of salvation, had not been all-encompassing enough. He started to reflect on passages like those in Jeremiah, where God's people are instructed to 'seek the welfare of the city', which he interpreted as seeking 'the common good, under God's care'. While previously he thought that 'meeting with Catholics' was an unimportant 'fringe thing', he now sees building good relationships with and reaching out to Catholics as 'an actual expression of the Gospel'. He believes other Presbyterian ministers share his old way of thinking and thinks this must change. 'We need to preach through issues like, what does it mean to love your enemy? What does it mean to do good to those who persecute you? We need to really spell it out, so people can say that this is actually part of our Christian faith.'

At the same time, John recognised that people who identify with loyalism and even the Orange Order feel increasingly marginalised by PCI.

> I have a wee neighbour who is in the Orange Order. He was talking about how a church wouldn't let them in to have their yearly service. He'd never been in the paramilitaries; he was a good wee guy. He said, 'John, no one wants us now.' Now, that's a church he has probably attended or been in and out of, and now he's not wanted. I don't know how you get round that, but that's a problem, too.

John also recognised that for Christianity to be relevant it not only had to be preached, but 'lived out' in culture and society.

> Christians are not only forgiven by God; they live out that forgiveness towards others. When Jesus said on the cross, 'Forgive them Father, for they know not what they do', he was speaking to ones who had judged, rejected, condemned and crucified him. The words, 'Father, forgive them' show the merciful heart

of God that Jesus carried towards his enemies. You can only forgive those who are guilty. That is why they need forgiveness. Loving your enemies means not allowing their sin of hating you and persecuting you to become a barrier to your embrace of them. Today our society is missing the power and beauty of forgiveness. The lack of forgiveness is a loss for healing and reconciliation.

'The paramilitaries were more supportive than the Presbyterian Church.'

Claire's husband was imprisoned for paramilitary offences, leaving her with a 3-month-old son. 'The paramilitaries came to me with a turkey every Christmas. I know it's only a token thing, but the church never was there. They never came with anything, not even to talk to you. The paramilitaries were more supportive than the Presbyterian Church.'

Claire went to a Presbyterian Sunday School, was married in the church, and had her son baptised there. She did not attend regularly during the early part of her marriage, but the minister visited after her husband was imprisoned. He did not offer support.

He started shouting and saying, 'He was standing in my church. I married him. Not so long ago he stood in my church and I christened his son. How dare he!' He said to me, 'You change your name and you change that child's name, and don't you ever have nothing to do with him ever again.' Then he prayed and he went away. I never seen him again. I wouldn't have went near him if I was dying, if he was going to save my life. His attitude wasn't Christian for starters. It wasn't even a human attitude.

She continued,

> He was just angry that this terrorist had the cheek to come into church. But Jesus would welcome people like that with open arms. Coming to church could change their lives. But not if they get shouted at and bawled at the way minsters did in them days. My sister and I, the minister we had when we were young, we were afraid of him, so we were. But it's not like that now, so it's not.

Claire grew up in a religiously mixed estate. When the Troubles began, her family was forced to leave. 'We were intimidated. They were going to set the whole place on fire. That's just what happened on both sides in those days.' The congregation she was part of then disbanded. 'It was within the war zone.' When she moved, the congregations in her new area helped people who had lost their homes by bringing them supplies. Claire recognised that people who attended church regularly, and had relatives in prison for paramilitary offences, received some support from ministers and congregations. She also appreciated the Quakers, who ran a café for the prison visitors.

Claire worked in a religiously mixed environment, and the Troubles impacted relationships with Catholics there. People withdrew into groups of their own religious background and avoided each other. 'You just wanted to be on your Protestant side. If I had been a Christian then, I might have been different. I might have tried to be a peacemaker and talk to people.'

Claire described herself now as having given her life to God.

> It's one of my prayers that no matter what religion you are, people should respect that and just let you get on with it. I don't know if reconciliation would be the right word, because they'll never be able to trust each other in this country. I hope this country never goes back to where we were, because there were so many lives ruined, so many lives lost senselessly.

'It was like a loyalist Jihad, that's what it was like.'

Joe was a teenager when he joined a paramilitary organisation. He lived in a working-class area that was targeted by republican paramilitaries. A family member was murdered. 'They were killing Protestants, bombing Protestants, abducting Protestants. I didn't see a war against the British; I saw a war against Protestants. They blew up every bar [in this area]. That is where working class Protestant men gathered. You could only assume that they wanted to kill Protestant working class men.'

Joe felt that political and religious leaders encouraged young men like him to resort to violence.

> Someone says, 'Liquidate the enemy.' What does that mean? That means: get guns and kill people. That's what people who were wearing [clerical] collars were saying – we have to arm ourselves. That's a hate preacher. That's radicalisation and I think it would be good if people could recognise that. It was like a loyalist Jihad, that's what it was like.

The words 'liquidate the enemy' were spoken by William
Craig, an Ulster Unionist Party politician and later
leader of the Vanguard party. Vanguard opposed power-
sharing with nationalists and had affiliations with loyalist
paramilitaries. Joe also said Rev. Ian Paisley incited
violence: 'What we thought as young people was that Free
Presbyterianism was really what Presbyterianism should
be. But Presbyterianism was weak and it didn't have a
political voice, whereas people like Dr Paisley crossed over
and said political things in a religious way: it was them or
us.'

As a child, Joe was sent to a Church of Ireland Sunday
School. When an older sister became Presbyterian, she
brought him to Presbyterian youth clubs. Joe did not
consider himself a Christian or go to church while he was
in a paramilitary organisation. In prison, he converted
to Christianity through the witness of his sister, prison
chaplains and other prisoners. 'A man gave me a Bible
and my sister and her husband would come and talk
to me and support me. They never tried to make me
Presbyterian. They just wanted me to have faith in Jesus
Christ. I realised I was a sinner and what I had done
was wrong and it separated me from God.' He also
remembered prison officers who were kind to him. 'They
were Christian men who were just trying to make a living,
keep a roof over their head. They would have said, "Here's
a good book I could recommend to you – ask someone to
get you that book." They didn't judge you for your past.'

Since his release from prison, Joe has worked in his
community 'to share the Gospel with people and to be
reconciled to people. I want to try and do some good
with my life, because I've been destructive. Not to redeem

myself – but to live the life I should have lived.' He said that those who engaged in violence on all sides should apologise. 'Lots of people say, "We shouldn't have done it, but here's the reasons why we did." Well, those reasons are never really justified. We thought like that at the time, but really it was wrong.'

Joe added that loyalist ex-prisoners 'felt let down by churches'. He agreed with them, saying that in some cases PCI seemed to sympathise more with republican ex-combatants than with loyalists. This was confirmed for him when he attended a conference on the Troubles organised by PCI.

> I listened to republicans tell of all the ills that were visited on them by the British state and by unionism. I saw lots of Presbyterian ministers nodding their heads in agreement. I don't see them nodding their heads in agreement when the same thing was done to working class Protestants. The RUC [Royal Ulster Constabulary] used and abused working class Protestants, too. I think a little bit of even-handedness wouldn't go amiss.

Joe was also concerned that republicans are 're-writing history'. He believed PCI was not challenging this republican narrative and was ignoring loyalists, because 'engaging with loyalists might get them a bad name'. Joe said PCI should try to understand loyalism. '[PCI] should have someone, or more than one person, especially set aside to be an outreach to loyalism. Not to be a missionary, but to listen. [Loyalists] are still being demonised as the bad guys in the Troubles. Everybody was a bad guy.'

*'[The churches] withdrew into their holy huddles
and their spiritual trenches and hid.'*

Timothy grew up in a working-class, interface area. He became increasingly angry about IRA violence, including the torture and murder of a relative 'who hadn't a bitter bone in his body'. His parents were devout. 'I was brought up in a Christian atmosphere and I had a happy childhood. My parents weren't bitter. They didn't hate Catholics. I never learnt that in the house – I learnt it outside the house.'

Timothy believed that during the Troubles, the churches 'withdrew into their holy huddles and their spiritual trenches and hid'. So, he stopped attending church.

> The only thing Christians were interested in was their own personal lives. They didn't give a hoot what went on in the country. I can't remember any Presbyterian minister who stepped out and put his neck on the line. The churches took sides. They didn't encourage violence, but it was still 'them and us'. In Protestant churches they were pro-unionist and in the Catholic Church they were pro-nationalist.

As a teenager, he joined a paramilitary organisation. In part, his decision was inspired by Rev. Ian Paisley. 'In their speeches, the Free Presbyterians and Paisley added fuel to the flames.' Timothy attended a rally in Belfast's Ormeau Park in 1972, where politician William Craig declared, 'If the politicians fail, it may be our job to liquidate the enemy.' He said, 'I'll never forget that day. They weren't talking about hockey sticks or baseball bats.'

Timothy was in prison when Paisley formed the Third Force (1981), a sort of militia of licensed firearms holders. Paisley led rallies where men waved firearms certificates.

> There was one fellow I met in prison. He was a member of the Third Force. He followed Paisley round marching through different villages. But the guns came in and he was caught. They washed their hands of him. Private armies were formed by those people. Those politicians and clergy would deny responsibility for any actions that was taken by the paramilitaries. But they played a part.

Timothy was born again in prison and is now devoted to a local congregation. After he was released from prison, 'There was individual Christians who helped me, but they were mainly family members. It wasn't the church. You were left to fend for yourself.' He attended several congregations after prison. 'Although I attended a few churches, yet, no matter where I went, I was never asked to get involved in any church activity. At times this left me discouraged and even disillusioned with some church leaders.'

Timothy said the churches can contribute to a better future only if they drop their preoccupation with 'getting more kids into Sunday School and more people into their church', and engage with the marginalised, including ex-combatants and those who are still using violence to control local communities. 'It might be distasteful to them, they might be sick to the pit of their stomach, but they have to. They must go and sit down with them and talk to them. Church leaders must do everything they can so that the Troubles never happen again.'

CHAPTER 6

Emergency Responders and Health Care Workers

People who worked in the emergency services and in health care were on the front lines of dealing with the death, injury and destruction of the Troubles. We spoke to doctors and nurses, other medical professionals, General Practitioners (GPs), people in the Ambulance and Fire Services, and a funeral director. Some worked in Belfast's Royal Victoria Hospital. The Royal was described as being located in a 'war zone', and was guarded day and night by police and army. Medical professionals there developed some of the world's most advanced techniques for dealing with traumatic injuries. Others worked in regional hospitals, general practices and border areas.

Emergency responders and health care workers were trained to treat all patients equally. This code was core to their professionalism and everyone we spoke with lived this as a matter of course. What they experienced made them angry or sad, but they 'just got on with it'. In the early days of the Troubles, their employers made no provision for their mental health – and rarely did their ministers or congregations acknowledge the stress they endured. They relied on prayer and the support of their medical colleagues. Many were leaders in their communities and tried to set a good example by living as 'normally' as possible in their everyday lives. Most who spoke about the Presbyterian Church in Ireland's (PCI) responses to the Troubles believed it had not done enough to promote peacemaking. Others said Rev. Ian Paisley had caused untold damage to their church, not to mention the wider society. Some spoke about how their work convinced them that Northern Ireland's future depends on forgiveness, while others claimed reconciliation was too much to ask.

'Armed police would have been guarding the doors in hospital.'

Hannah began nursing in Belfast in the late 1970s. 'Armed police would have been guarding the doors in hospital. That was just the norm.' After one bomb attack, the perpetrator and one of the victims were treated on the same ward. 'It was only an eight-bed ward. That didn't pose a problem because everyone was treated equal.' She was on duty the night Bobby Sands was brought in during his hunger strike. 'I remember going for our tea at the canteen and coming back and the walls were just lined with police and army.'

When she was a teenager, Hannah's father, who served part-time in the security forces, was injured in an off-duty attack. He died a few years later. There were other victims in her congregation. 'In our church, the importance of prayer and taking your feelings to God were emphasised. Treating everybody with respect and dignity is what the church teaches.' She translated that message into her nursing. 'I always felt compassionate and treated people equally and fairly. If you were worried about something, you took it to God in prayer.'

Hannah's congregation did not talk about the Troubles. 'They were private people. Everybody was hurting at that stage. There was fear as well.' She appreciated her minister's support and felt ministers' own mental health was neglected. 'I don't know that there was much support for them as ministers. I know as a nurse we didn't really have any support groups where we would have been asked how we were coping. There was no occupational health or anything like that in those days.'

Hannah saw the church as a restraining influence during the Troubles. She was proud her father had been involved with her congregation's Boys' Brigade (BB).

The Boys' Brigade [BB] was a great way for young men to stay out of trouble, due to teaching Christian values to boys. There was a lot of young men who could have got involved in violence or been swayed to join [paramilitary groups]. Although the BB was not the only restraining influence, it was one organisation that kept some people from joining. Even though daddy's dead over forty years, when you meet them now they say, 'The times we had, the joy we had, from the BB.' I love to hear his name and that he's still being thought of. He was very important to them at that stage of their lives.

'All blood's red. There's no orange or green blood.'

Philip worked for more than thirty years in the pathology laboratory of a regional hospital near the border.

During the Troubles a lot of what happened here, shootings, bombings – those came to us. The blood transfusion end was very important. We were there as soon as we got the phone call. The first thing you did was check your blood stock. Then you ran over to casualty and spoke to the doctors, to the anaesthetist – he was the one setting up the blood.

What Philip remembers the most is victims' families. 'The thing I recall from it is the anguish. You would have had relatives in. The people who carried out the things didn't hear the shouting, the cursing, the screaming. We always used to say: "The people who did it don't see this."'

During the most violent years,

Every month there was two or three major incidents [to deal with in hospital]. There was an atmosphere almost as if you were under siege. You got on with your life on the surface, but there was that undercurrent of anxiety. You never really knew if a bomb would go off. But in a strange way, you didn't worry about it too much.

The laboratory staff was split almost evenly between Protestants and Catholics. 'Our boss had a rule that the tearoom was a place for laughing and joking. There was no political discussion allowed. The thing we used to say was: "All blood's red. There's no orange or green blood."'

Philip was in his early twenties when the Troubles began.

You just got on with life. There was a certain amount of personal defiance, too. The people who hunker down and get on with it are the people that run the country. Even when there were shootings outside churches, you were that wee bit wary, but that didn't stop you from going to your church. The churches just went about their business.

Philip appreciated 'people like Rev. Ken Newell' who reached out to Catholics during the Troubles. But he believed that many in PCI were not ready to 'push forward'. He thought Protestants should realise that 'in the old days we were wrong; this superiority over Catholics was wrong – and vice versa. We all worship the one God. I don't think they'll get very far telling everybody they need to be saved. There also must be an element of forgiveness. You have to recognise where you were wrong.'

*'I hope by our actions we did as much as
we could to help people in dark times.'*

Helen worked for many years as a GP in a border area, serving rural towns and villages.

We were seeing a lot of the effects of the Troubles: injuries, long-term illnesses. I can think of one elderly farmer whose only son had been shot in front of him, the son who was going to take over the farm. That father never really recovered. Then we were getting people who belonged to the UDR [Ulster Defence Regiment] who were living in very difficult circumstances, always watchful of who was about, what was under their car. Some of them came to breaking point and that was when we were called. One man who belonged to the security forces was stationed in a town where their premises were constantly besieged, but they were required to do regular patrols in vehicles. One afternoon he came to me visibly shaking; shortly before his vehicle had been blown up. He said, 'I have to go back in the morning and do the same thing all over again.' He stuck that for decades.

Understanding of and access to mental health care was 'very poor' at that time.

> If you mentioned psychiatric help, some people had misconceptions about what could be provided and the stigma it would have for them within their workplace or family circle. There were no community mental health teams in the way there are nowadays. Unfortunately, to try and see someone over the most critical and difficult crisis you often had to use medication. But you knew you hadn't the back-up in the health service and in the forces to cope with the tremendous workload.

Helen's hometown was bombed many times. Her mother's house sustained significant damage on several occasions. One explosion happened while Helen was at work. When she heard about it, she rushed home.

> I found a policeman and said, 'Is it possible I could go and see if my folks were still alive?' After a while he came back, and he took me up. I saw the devastation of our house. Then down the back garden I found my mother and sister-in-law and the baby. The baby wasn't expecting the bang, naturally, and it stopped breathing. Her mother had the presence of mind to

turn the child upside down and give it a bang on the back and it started breathing again.

The attacks did not make her angry, but sad – and grateful that in her case, the damage was limited to bricks and mortar rather than flesh and blood.

She was reminded of the danger every time she came home from work in the evenings. To curtail car bombings, police erected barriers on the road. This meant she couldn't get her car home. 'I used to park my car in a friend's house [beyond the barriers] and walk half a mile with my doctor's bag at midnight or one o'clock in the morning.' Later, the barriers could be opened at night, but Helen had to stop at a regional police station to tell them when she would be arriving at a barrier, so they could let her through.

Helen recalled that one Presbyterian minister in her area 'was very much tuned in with what was going on and was one of those people who was alongside his flock'. He contacted her practice when he thought people needed professional help coping with what had happened to them and asked for a doctor to visit them. Helen said it was difficult for PCI to do much publicly, especially with Rev. Ian Paisley criticising its every move.

It's very hard to see how the Presbyterian Church could have done much more apart from saying, 'We're with you, we're thinking of you, and we're praying for you.' Those who did try, in the background, to meet with IRA [Irish Republican Army] people were vilified. They were trying to be peacemakers, but at that time the anger in people's hearts was such that those people were not given support. There were people [inside and outside PCI] who supported Paisley and they felt there was to be no compromise.

Some members of Helen's congregation led the Ulster Worker's Council strike (1974) in her area, a protest against the Sunningdale Agreement and a perceived sell-out to Irish nationalism.

We had one or two rather militant people in our congregation who set themselves up as the people to lead the action. I was working [in another town], and I was approached. Petrol was rationed by them, and we were being told the government didn't matter, they were taking over. We were coming out of church. They said, 'Doctor, do you need any petrol?' I said, 'No, thank you. If I run out of petrol, I will cycle to work rather than have you dictate to me what I'm to do.'

This act of defiance reflected the life Helen lived, day-by-day. 'We were obliged to minister to everybody: our Catholic patients as well as our Protestant patients. I hope by our actions we did as much as we could to help people in dark times.'

'It was hard not to be angered.'

Janis began nursing in the Royal in the mid-1970s. Although the soldiers guarding the Royal were there to protect staff and patients, she was especially nervous when she worked in the cardiac ward.

If there's a cardiac arrest, somebody's going to come flying out that door with an arrest trolley. Soldiers were sitting there with guns with live ammunition on their knees. I used to think, 'If those doors swing open, their first instinct is going to be to shoot.' I used to say to them, 'Please don't be trigger happy.' We're talking about 18-year-old boys, children really, sitting with live ammunition in what was a war zone for them.

Janis was often angered by what she saw, because the pain inflicted had been intentional. 'It was hard not to be angered. Particularly, policemen that I felt were just doing a job. Equally there were taxi drivers who, just because they were Catholic, were lured to areas and shot. I nursed soldiers in intensive care who'd had limbs blown off. For a long time, the smell of flesh stayed with you.'

Janis lived in a Protestant town outside Belfast and people in the congregation didn't talk much about the Troubles. She was helped by her minister's preaching on forgiveness. But there wasn't much recognition that her job was stressful.

Looking back, I would have been quite depressed. At that stage nobody acknowledged that – you got on with it. I had a husband who was a Christian and he would have supported me. We would have prayed together and been involved in prayer and Bible study in the church. It was a matter of getting through it with your own personal faith.

Janis said PCI should have done more to contribute to peacemaking. 'We didn't reach out as we should have. We just kept doing what we had done.' She added that people like Rev. Ken Newell, who was active in peacemaking and ecumenical initiatives, should have been supported. 'Some people didn't like what he was doing because they saw it as threatening their Protestantism, rather than seeing it as a way forward for compromise.'

Now, she thinks PCI could help create spaces for 'recognising other people's genuine pain' and encouraging forgiveness.

> I have been forgiven in Christ so that is not something I can withhold from somebody else. If somebody is seeking reconciliation without repentance – that's a difficult one. I wouldn't have reconciliation with God without repentance. There has to be an acknowledgment of the hurt before we can begin to build the bridge that allows us to move forward together.

'There was bombs left at the door.'

Harold served forty-three years in the fire service. He responded to countless tragedies. 'The fire service would have had lots of trouble, so we had. There was bombs left at the door. There was a terrible lot of trouble round here: it's a border town, you see.'

Harold worked another job in addition to the fire service. When there was an incident, a siren blew in the town. 'We jumped out and were away. It wasn't, I suppose, easy.' He described how part of his job was 'lifting the fragments of bodies and putting them into a bag'. Harold was part of the large-scale response to the Enniskillen bomb in 1987. 'A real disaster. People lying everywhere just.' Despite the horror, he believed it was important to do his part to preserve life and property.

Harold attended a congregation of about eighty families. Among them, there were twenty people who served in the Royal Ulster Constabulary (RUC), UDR or emergency services. 'There was quite a lot of lads maimed for life.' The congregation 'helped them out as much as they could'. They didn't talk about the Troubles. 'We just sort of adjusted. It was bad enough and it could have been worse.' He added that his minister 'didn't take any part in it'; meaning he didn't address 'politics'. Harold thought this was the correct approach. 'We got through it anyway.'

'It was a baptism of fire.'

After qualifying as a doctor, Brett had been working only a few days in Accident and Emergency (A&E) in the Royal when he attended a civilian with life-threatening injuries from a terrorist attack. 'That boy survived despite us to be perfectly honest. We were qualified a matter of a few months. It was a baptism of fire.'

Brett had to learn on his feet.

In most war zones, by the time you got patients to a hospital they had died. Whereas in this situation, the war zone was outside the hospital, so patients were getting to the hospital. People would come from all over the world to see what was happening in the Royal because they knew that's where the cutting edge of emergency medicine and major trauma was going on.

There was a British Army regiment on duty at all hours to protect staff and patients. Yet Brett recalled an incident when a soldier standing outside the Royal was shot by an IRA sniper. 'A doctor had to crawl out on hands and knees and drag this soldier in.'

Brett's thinking about Troubles-related issues was shaped by the Evangelical Contribution on Northern Ireland (ECONI), a special-interest organisation dedicated to helping evangelicals respond to Northern Ireland's political divisions. ECONI critiqued how Northern Ireland's evangelical tradition had justified anti-Catholicism, and encouraged evangelicals to get involved in peacemaking. He was part of a Catholic–Protestant group that met locally and used ECONI resources to discuss religious and political issues.

Brett described the Troubles as a 'common evil' and lamented that many people were caught up in the violence. He was aware of 'many stories of God's grace' working to heal people who had suffered. But he doesn't underestimate the difficulty of reconciliation. 'I was never personally affected [by bereavement or injury], either my family or myself, so it's easy for me to stand high and mighty and have all this wonderful theological thinking. But I need to be sympathetic to those folk whose hurt has been immense.'

He then told a story about a soldier he treated in A&E.

He was a young guy. He lost both legs and one arm. It was my last day in A&E. I moved to the surgical ward so I dealt with him there, and then for the next three months I dressed his wounds. It was one of the hardest things I've had to do. We became friends, not deep friends, through very difficult days. So for me to preach the Gospel of good news to him: I know it's not hollow, but gosh, I need to be sensitive. To

reconcile him to somebody else that's a big, big task.
I couldn't do it. It would have to be a divine thing
that would bring him to a point of forgiving whoever
it was that blew him up.

'It was our job to keep normality normal.'

As teenagers in the 1970s, Jeffrey and his friends organised
themselves into a venture scouts group and worked to
qualify for the Duke of Edinburgh Award. As part of that
process, they volunteered with the ambulance service
and as orderlies in the local hospital. Their first night on
ambulance duty, there were two shootings and two car
accidents. 'Our first night we were out dressed in civvies.
Then they decided to put us in white coats. I maintain it
was to make us a better target!' he laughed. Jeffrey said
they were so young that, 'We never thought much of it.
Your job was to patch the guy up and get him into the
ambulance and get him back for treatment as quickly as
possible, in a dignified way.'

As hospital orderlies, the teenagers helped with
administration and other tasks when there were
emergencies. 'You wouldn't be able to do things like that
now. Yet we felt we were helping. We weren't in the way;
we weren't a hindrance.'

Jeffrey was later a teacher. He worked in a town
with a strong loyalist paramilitary presence and taught
several subjects, including Religious Education (RE). He
developed a real fondness for the people and stayed more
than three decades.

You had a job to do – and you just got on with it. You
had to maintain an aloofness from [paramilitarism]

because you couldn't afford to be in their pocket. You will never control them, but I think you can avoid yourself being totally under their control. I'm sure there are a number of boys who I've taught that have been in [paramilitaries]. By the time I finished teaching, [local people] knew you, knew that you'd been faithful and reliable to the school. I think sometimes that's all that's necessary: you have to prove that you're prepared to sit it out and be there for them and with them.

Jeffrey admitted once getting into 'trouble' for what he said in a RE class about the Drumcree dispute. He displayed the symbols Orangemen wear on their sashes and drew a Bible and a cross on the blackboard. He asked the pupils if any were Orangemen. Some raised their hands but admitted they did not go to church. He told them, 'You boys say you're Orangemen and you represent me. You don't represent anything I stand for. I would not be an Orangeman because you boys are not standing for what is right. You're standing for an Orange idea that is contrary to the symbols you're wearing.' Many parents – not just those sympathetic to the Orange Order – could have felt he overstepped the line. But 'it was a risk I was prepared to take'.

During the Troubles, Jeffrey saw his role as a citizen as carrying on with life as normally as possible. 'There were lots of people who we'll never know about, unsung heroes. It was our job to keep normality normal: in faith, in work, socialising in the town, shopping. Because if you didn't, then you were failing in your job. Not just as a Christian, but as a human being.'

*'Some families actually turned to the church
because they'd nobody else to turn to.'*

As a funeral director, Stephen attended the scene of many Troubles-related incidents to collect bodies for burial. Like other first responders, Stephen could be called away to his duties in the middle of the night. While he provided funerals for both Protestants and Catholics, he was also contracted to the security forces. 'The police told me I could be under threat because I was working for the security forces.'

That threat felt especially real after one horrific incident. 'It was about two in the morning. I went with my colleagues and it was a very hostile situation. There were a lot of police there and a lot of people from the local area who hadn't taken too kindly to the security forces. There were missiles and bottles and bricks being thrown.' The aftermath of the incident was broadcast on television.

> It was widely seen by a lot of people [on television] that we were doing the removals. I got a call from one of the local inspectors saying they had concerns for my personal safety. It meant I had to be very vigilant in the mornings when I was taking my children to school. I had to check under my car [for bombs].

Stephen recalled planning funerals with grieving families. He knew many personally. 'If you have somebody that's lived a good life and they've come to an end at eighty or ninety years, you are a professional when you do that funeral. But when it's someone young [who has been murdered] it's difficult.'

He attended church regularly. 'I did pray every night that my family would be safe. I prayed the same in the morning again, that they would be safe.' His long and irregular hours put a strain on family life. 'It had to be done and somebody had to do it. You just had to get on with it.'

Stephen never received pastoral care or counselling, but he organised counselling and a 'grief share' programme through his funeral home which catered for bereaved families, doctors, nurses and ambulance and fire service workers. 'We took it on ourselves to do that. Could the churches have done that? I don't know. I thought the church could have run something like that and done a wee bit more that way.'

He said local ministers and congregations were always helpful when planning funerals. He observed that tragic events could either push people towards or away from the church. 'Some families actually turned to the church because they'd nobody else to turn to. They become Christians then and realised how much they needed the church. Others turned away and went in a different direction. I would have seen people who turned to alcohol after a very bad incident.'

'You just got on with it.'

Liz started nursing in the Royal in 1975. 'By the time I started, the big, big bombs were trailing off a little bit – it wasn't just as awful.' Her duties still could be harrowing, especially when she worked in casualty.

I remember [an incident] when the doors flung open and there was two soldiers. Both had been shot in the

head. One died in the main room. I remember hushed
tones that he was gone. I still feel emotional about it
– even today. The other fella, I remember standing
packing the gunshot wound with gauze, packing the
side of his head that was messy. At the time it was
okay, you just got on with it. His hand brushed against
mine when we were moving him from the trolley, and
he had a wedding ring on and I remember thinking:
'His wife has no idea where he is at the minute. She
has no idea what's happening to him.' That actually
felt like a privilege that I was there to try and do my
wee bit to help. Then I went up with him to theatre
and he died there.

Liz felt 'ashamed' that British soldiers were required to
guard the Royal. 'I remember walking past them and
feeling ashamed of us – of Northern Ireland people – that
were taking these lives.'

She worked with nurses of all backgrounds. They
didn't talk about politics, or even about what they were
experiencing.

There was no talk about Catholic/Protestant/IRA. It
was an unwritten policy that you just got on with it.
There was no talk of us getting counselling for the
things we saw or did. It was the nature of the work –
you were busy and then the next day came and there
was something else to do, so you didn't spend a long
time reflecting on things.

Her faith helped.

It was a case of walking your Christian path and living
your Christian life. I've found the Lord a great source

of comfort. Not that there was a whole lot of answers to questions, but just to know He was in control. My Christianity was a great help to me for day-to-day living. I don't know how girls that wouldn't have been Christians got through it.

Liz has no sympathy for the IRA, but she has studied Irish history and gained a greater understanding of 'British imperialism, and how they lorded it over the Irish people'. She said Ulster Protestants had treated Catholics unfairly, adding,

I can understand the civil rights movement but not the violence. With self-examination comes an understanding that you're not always right and maybe there's somebody else can have an element of truth on their side too. Now, from a Christian point of view, I can see how our kingdom isn't Protestant or Catholic, Britain or Ireland. Our kingdom is God's kingdom. So, if it was a united Ireland and the Gospel was free to move around, that would be okay.

'You could actually feel the evilness at a scene.'

Paul worked for twenty-eight years in the Ambulance Service, responding to countless incidents. 'We were first on the scene before doctors and nurses would have arrived. You'd look at somebody and within a second you could say whether they're going to survive. It was an awful thing to do, but you walked away from them and dealt with people who were survivable. We lifted the survivable ones and went to hospital.'

Paul took some solace from his belief that God would one day judge the perpetrators. 'I always thought, the boy who did this, he's going to meet God sometime. The devil has got a hold of these people and they're brainwashed into what they're doing. You could actually feel the evilness at a scene.'

Paul also belonged to the UDR. He said joining was 'the done thing' in his area. 'You were expected to join. I was proud I joined but I was relieved after the twenty years not to have had to fire a shot in anger.'

At the time, it was believed that the IRA had a plan to put one person from the security forces in the graveyard in every Protestant church along the border.

> We'd no-one in our church graveyard from the security forces. It actually started to scare me. I'd be looking at the members of the security forces every Sunday, and I was thinking, 'Who's it going to be, who's it going to be?' But then something happened in a different town and one of the people was reared here, so they were buried in the church. I actually had a sigh of relief.

Counselling was not available. 'We counselled ourselves. You'd go home into bed, but you couldn't sleep because your mind was so active. Now, there's no one to say thank you for what we were doing. The churches were lazy. They prayed for the security forces and the Ambulance Service, but it wasn't a deep personal thing.'

He thought some ministers were reluctant to offer support, for fear of causing offence.

> We're proud people. We don't like to talk about it. We don't like to let ourselves down. So, the ministers

just go through the formalities. There's not the deep follow up there could have been. A lot of ministers would have the attitude, 'If there's anything wrong, they'll come to me', rather than going out and giving a Christian witness.

Paul added that the statements the churches made about the Troubles were bland and ineffective. 'You could near write them yourself. They were impersonal, an official statement and that was it. [The churches] never done anything that would rattle cages.'

'Working and living in the Royal could be scary.'

Barbara grew up in a rural town in the Republic and started nursing in the Royal when she was seventeen and a half years old. 'Prior to coming to Belfast, I had no understanding of what the Troubles were. I had known there were disturbances in Londonderry and other places in '69 but it didn't impact. It really did impact as a student nurse.' Student nurses lived in rooms in the grounds of the Royal.

Everybody was learning on the job and you came to expect the unexpected. You went to work and came back and had a cup of tea with your friends and talked over the day and that was it. Regardless of the atrocities that you were dealing with there was no such thing as counselling. Looking back on it all now, there was nothing normal about it – but the abnormal became normal.

Nurses supported each other. 'Most of us, I believe, walked away without any PTSD issues because we talked to each other.' In addition to dealing with serious injuries and deaths, 'Working and living in the Royal could be scary. There was always an army and police presence and a number of serious incidents occurred within the hospital and grounds.'

Barbara worked most weekends and only attended church in her home town on her weekend off. 'In those days – and I have thought about this – I do not ever remember any church I attended, any responses being made to the Troubles. I don't think people knew how to deal with it. Maybe my church [in the Republic] was too far away.' She recalled Church of Ireland Archbishop Robin Eames promoting peacemaking and said some Moderators and 'individuals made huge differences'. In the late 1980s, Barbara attended church on Sunday evenings. Her faith wasn't as strong then as it is now, but 'even if I wasn't too close to God, I would always have prayed'.

For Barbara, reconciliation is 'working together for the common good'. But she feared that 'Northern Ireland has not grown up enough' to have a conversation about reconciliation. 'I'm not sure that reconciliation where there is no feeling of remorse is actually the right word. I think you must feel remorse to reconcile.'

'I prayed God would see us through the night.'

Wendy worked for forty-two years as a night manager nurse in a regional hospital. 'It was humming with activity during the Troubles. There wasn't a night went past but it was just bedlam in the department.' During emergencies it was all hands on deck. 'I was responsible for all the hospital. If they needed help, I rolled up my sleeves.

Regardless of how hectic we were, God gave us the ability to get through the workload by morning – and may I say without any mistakes.'

Wendy recalled her sadness when attending incidents.

On one occasion, I went round the corner to help and lo and behold, this UDR sergeant had come in and he recognised me, and spoke my name. I could see the smile on his face; he was elated to know somebody after being injured. But he lay back and died. His aorta was ruptured. It was all very sad and I had to be stronger in my faith.

The Troubles made Wendy think 'a lot about God'. Thinking about God made her aware of the need to show 'kindness and love' in her profession: to patients, grieving relatives and fellow staff.

Staff faced further pressures from politicians who came to the hospital after serious incidents, demanding information; and from the media. 'You would get the intrusion of photographers trying to come in while people were in theatres, pushing their way in. I remember grabbing a camera off a photographer and refused to give it to him. Fortunately, the police came in and took the camera. I just carried on.'

Wendy's commute included roads with culverts under them, which made them attractive for those planting bombs; and housing estates where there could be rioting. 'There's nights we had diversions and had to go different ways to get to work. I always got there safely, thank the Lord. When I travelled to my work I would have prayed and sang hymns. I prayed God would see us through the night.'

Wendy believed the churches should have worked together more during the Troubles and this should be their priority today. 'There was a man, Mr [Ian] Paisley. He's beside the point. He went off on his own and others followed him. But I feel the other churches should have got together with the priests. Talking is very, very important and you have to listen to one another's views.'

When asked about reconciliation, Wendy admitted it would be very hard, responding by telling stories about two victims. The first was a teenage relative, who had been shot in a case of mistaken identity. The family was so frightened that they left the area, while the killer now walks free. The second was another relative, a policeman who 'was shot through the head and was a vegetable lying in the hospital where I worked, for over two decades'. She described how one Christmas she went into his room and saw the letters his children had written him, telling him what presents they had received. 'The tears rolled down my cheeks and I thought: The poor fella, he doesn't even know.' His wife, who didn't drive, visited him every day. 'She had to walk to a bus, go to the hospital, and that ritual back home again, every day of her life. Now, would she have an answer for reconciliation? I do not know. For it was a living death all those years.'

*'Playing a hymn on the piano would
just bring me back emotionally.'*

As a young medical student, Heidi had just settled down in the library at the Royal when she heard gunshots. 'Get down!' someone shouted. Heidi scrambled for shelter. 'The mortuary was just beside the library and one of the mortuary attendants had been shot dead. That was the first impact of the Troubles on me.'

Heidi qualified in the late 1970s and became a GP in a border area. No members of her family were killed or injured, so she considers herself 'one of the lucky ones'. Much of her work has been helping others cope. 'I have certified people [dead] who have been killed in the Troubles. But it's dealing with the families later that impacts my work.'

Heidi's patients have reacted very differently to tragedies. Some have 'moved on', and others need psychiatric support decades later. It's not always obvious why some people fare better than others. One patient was injured in a gun attack. When the man who shot him was released from jail, 'He had to see him face-to-face walking round the streets. But he had accepted that he had been punished for what he'd done and was able to accept it. I'm always amazed at how people react to tragedies in their life. You just have to listen and be there and help them.'

Heidi often made house calls late at night. She said her 'worst problem' was the dangerous driving of smugglers. 'Their lorries would have no lights on and they would go straight down the road. You had to just pull over.' Any vehicles on the road in the wee hours aroused the suspicion of the police. 'I was alright until I changed my car – then the police stopped me: "Oh, it's you, doctor. You got a new car." As soon as they knew my car, I never had any problems.' Once, Heidi attended a sick child in a republican estate. Shortly after she drove out, 'This car came along and cut down in front of me and four army men stopped me. That was the most frightening thing I ever came across. Once they realised I was a doctor and was visiting a patient, there was no problem.'

Heidi managed the emotional toll of her work by taking walks, reading the Bible and playing the piano. 'Playing a hymn on the piano would just bring me back emotionally.' Local clergy from several denominations would ask her how she was doing and 'give me the opportunity to talk if I wanted'. But 'I found I was better talking to colleagues who were working in the same conditions. I was the one trying to give counselling to people who were suffering.'

Right now, Heidi thinks the task of reconciliation is 'too big'. For her, 'We have to have forgiveness and resilience. Resilience is where people – even though they're facing difficult situations – find something within themselves to move on. With reconciliation, it has to be individual before the community can do it.'

'If you have confidence in God's sovereignty, it does help.'

Husband and wife Thomas and Tracy worked as a surgical registrar and anaesthetist in several hospitals during the Troubles, including the Royal. Thomas said, 'We used to meet between work and hand over the children.' Tracy chimed in, 'We'd write notes on the kitchen table.' Thomas added, 'But at least you had someone who understood at home. At the time you are busy – you go into automatic mode. You don't theorise on the day. But if you have confidence in God's sovereignty, it does help in the time afterwards when you reflect on it.'

Tracy told the interviewer, 'When Thomas said you were coming today, I said, "I don't remember anything of the Troubles – I've just blocked it out." All I know is that I would not want to return there – it was absolutely horrendous.' Yet during the interview, Tracy recalled an incident when she went to casualty 'to check everything was clear'. It was during the changeover period so incoming staff were being briefed. 'A guy had been put down in fractures to wait. When I pulled the curtains aside, it was a guy who had been in my brother's class at school. He was a policeman. He was lying there with both legs off, just bleeding into the bed. I remember putting on tourniquets and running for help. The ambulance men had put him in there. They were just so used to seeing maimed people that [they assumed he'd] be seen in a minute.' While the policeman lived, he died young.

Thomas was on duty in the Royal the night of the bomb in the La Mon restaurant in 1978. Tracy had been working during the day and had just returned home when she heard the sirens of emergency vehicles.

> I prayed for him because I knew something big was on. You always prayed for safety for the people who go out, too, because the ambulance guys and the paramedics could have been victims of another bomb. When you were left at home not able to do anything, you would sit and pray for those who were going to the front line.

Both believed PCI should have stood up to Rev. Ian Paisley. Thomas said, 'The church was terribly defensive because of Paisleyism. It pushed them in directions they probably didn't want to go and shouldn't have gone.' He added that some of his family 'became rabid Free Presbyterians and didn't speak to us for years because we didn't join'.

Both said PCI could benefit from a better understanding of grace, adding that it was easier for them to contemplate forgiveness because they had not lost relatives during the Troubles. Thomas said, '[PCI] were too timid in being gracious and in promoting what Jesus said, "If you won't forgive, you can't be forgiven." We're all undeserving of grace, so we have to forget about what we deserve, about revenge and retribution.'

CHAPTER 7

Quiet Peacemakers

Some Presbyterians responded to the Troubles by working for peace. We have called them 'quiet peacemakers', because their labours were often behind the scenes, unnoticed and unappreciated except by those whose lives they helped change for the better. For some, careers as youth workers, social and community workers, or schoolteachers meant they dealt with the impact of violence and paramilitarism on the young and the vulnerable. Others owned small businesses and saw their role as maintaining normality in the chaos, welcoming and respecting everyone. Still others became involved in peace activism through para-church organisations like Evangelical Contribution on Northern Ireland (ECONI) or Corrymeela; or in their own congregations. They believed being a peacemaker should be central to their Christian witness in a violent and religiously divided society. Many described deep relationships with Catholics, whose faith inspired them. We also spoke with people who participated in or were employed on the Presbyterian Church in Ireland's (PCI) Peacemaking Programme (2006–9); or who served as 'peace agents', people who were designated to lead peacemaking in their local congregations.

Some quiet peacemakers felt their congregations affirmed their work. But most reported that neither their congregation nor PCI supported peacemaking. One woman said that out of more than 500 Presbyterian congregations, only 'about ten' created meaningful partnerships with a Catholic parish. Others noted that most congregations did not have peace agents or peace groups.[15] Some felt women's contributions were overlooked. Others said PCI had not even supported its most prominent peacemakers, like Revs Lesley Carroll, John Dunlop, Ken Newell and Ruth Patterson, among others. Quiet peacemakers persisted because they believed churches could contribute to peace. But for this to be fully realised, they believed churches must make peacemaking central to their missions, rather than treating it as an 'optional add-on'.

*'Children [were] pulled out of youth clubs and
taken away for punishment beatings.'*

Lindsay Conway has been a youth worker and social worker for faith-based and secular organisations for over forty years. He was ordained as an elder in West Church in Bangor in 1979 and has been secretary for PCI's Council for Social Witness since 2002.

In the early days of the Troubles, churches opened their doors for people displaced from their homes or affected by rioting. 'My congregation, Megain Memorial, was in the middle of the Newtownards Road in East Belfast, so it was open at night to take all and sundry. But you would have had people objecting to coming into contact with Catholics from Short Strand, even if they were young mums with babies.' He contrasted this to his professional perspective as a social worker. 'I couldn't have thought about what denomination or what religion they were. You had to provide a service.'

Lindsay was involved with the YMCA (national chair and president) and accompanied groups to Corrymeela. 'Organisations could take risks because they weren't denominations. The churches didn't embrace us in the early days.' He believed PCI focused too much on saving individual souls and had to be gradually convinced to prioritise peacemaking and other forms of social witness like work with drug addicts and ex-prisoners. He also worked on a Community Relations Commission programme that took young people from different backgrounds abroad. 'That went well, but we failed with regards to the long-term benefits because wee Jimmy and Paddy couldn't play together when they came back.' He attended weekly inter-church prayer meetings, and even a youth mass in St Peter's Cathedral. 'I was getting hammered personally for attending mass, even in the media.' That year, he stood up at the national assembly of YMCAs of Ireland and, 'I posed the question: "Have we ever seriously thought why God is not answering our prayers for peace?" Then I posed the question: "Why are we such a bad witness?"'

Lindsay's work within social work and the Rathgael Training School made him more aware than most of how the conflict was impacting disadvantaged young people.

Young people were fodder to the paramilitaries. They used young people, children really, because the perception was that their penalties would be less than adults who would be caught for the same thing. Some churches had youth clubs, but even in a youth club, children could be drawn into things. There were cases of children being pulled out of youth clubs and taken away for punishment beatings. The churches didn't respond or were unable to respond to the paramilitaries' impact on young people.

Among those Lindsay worked with, 'It's well into double figures those who were murdered or killed doing something they shouldn't have been doing. I would stand at another graveside, thinking, "This is just unbelievable."' A boy Lindsay worked with was murdered on his birthday. 'I used to meet that wee mum when I was out and about and every time she said, "Remember that night you took me down to identify the body." She just lived with that.' Lindsay was often on call and when his phone rang,

> I prayed some of the most un-Godly prayers: 'What am I going to do, Lord?' You came across some terrible stuff. Your priority was to get this family somewhere safe, get this kid medically looked after, protected and moved. We were having to get permission of the paramilitaries for people to go out to funerals. But you couldn't have done it any other way and we weren't heroes.

Though the work was taxing, Lindsay felt it was his calling. 'I remember one time the phone rang again, and I had to go out to deal with a situation. I remembered the words from the Bible, "You're about your Father's business." That was my lightbulb moment.'

Between 2002 and 2012, Lindsay was the Presbyterian representative on 'Journey Towards Healing', a partnership between the churches, the Northern Ireland Association for Mental Health, and the Victims Unit. It focused on helping ministers cope with secondary trauma.

> We really underestimated the impact on clergy relating to funerals, to interaction with paramilitaries. If you get a phone call from your church member, 'I've been threatened with a knee-capping', it's not normal. You don't get training for that in Union Theological College. When you started talking to ministers, you learned that no-one had ever talked to them about these things.

Lindsay said PCI had been 'balanced but very cautionary' in its response to the Troubles.

> Under good relations and peacemaking we have done things that have been important. When you compare that to what individuals have done, like Rev. Ray Davey, Rev. John Dunlop or Rev. Ken Newell – PCI has benefitted from their work. But to have tried to bring the whole church was difficult. If we'd made a resolution in the 1980s or 1990s that every Presbyterian congregation twin with a Catholic congregation, there would have been absolute mayhem. That's just being slightly flippant. As a denomination we are now far more understanding of other denominations.

'It's better to have a little candle shining in the darkness.'

Isobel was a schoolteacher in a town where many were killed during the Troubles. Some incidents had multiple casualties. She attended funerals and visited families after bereavements. Decades after one of the worst incidents,

'I still remember the next morning going into school, the silence when I walked into class and the faces turned round to me as if to say, how can this be made right? There was a real feeling of helplessness.'

Isobel oversaw the school assembly that morning. 'School had to finish early every day that week because there were funerals. How do you bring some sort of Christian comfort into that situation? We had a reading and a hymn, and I said a very simple prayer. Many of the children knew people that had died or were injured. Everyone was still in shock.'

Weeks later, a schoolgirl came to Isobel distraught because during the incident, she had run away from a friend who had asked her to help look for her little brother, who was lost in the mayhem. 'You were trying to talk through how what she'd done was understandable, and about God's forgiveness of her in her frailty. A lot of the time I was listening and just trying to be with people, reassuring them that God loved them, that God was with them in their sorrow, and that God wept as they wept.'

Isobel had grown up in a predominantly Protestant town, but even after living in a mixed town for more than a decade, she didn't have many Catholic friends. After this incident,

I felt a real sense of guilt about why this had happened. Part of the reason was that we were two separate communities. I hadn't engaged with Catholics, talked with them about the important things. I hadn't brought my faith to bear on the situation in Northern Ireland or looked at my responsibility as a Christian in terms of reaching out to the other community.

Isobel joined an inter-church group. 'We went to each other's churches and talked with each other about what we saw. Over time, we engaged with people from Sinn Féin, to try and understand their position.' When this group folded, she joined another, and remains involved. 'In my own spiritual journey, I have found my engagement with folk from the Catholic tradition has enriched my spiritual life.' She is disappointed that the inter-church group remains small. She feels let down when her fellow Presbyterians are uninterested. 'We organise things and people don't come. There's no hostility – there's more apathy now, really. We wonder if we should fold, but the feeling is, it's better to have a little candle shining in the darkness.'

Isobel said PCI had not always shown leadership during the Troubles. In her view, this was due to PCI struggling to keep its diverse membership united. 'In every congregation you have people like me who want to engage with folk from other denominations; and you have folk who are not comfortable with that or who are still suffering from the Troubles. We've managed to accommodate these differences, but only by ignoring the fact that people have different perspectives.' She also thought Moderators were prevented from showing leadership due to their short, one-year term, which meant Moderators who wanted to engage with other denominations didn't have adequate opportunities.

For her, this signalled that,

The Presbyterian Church has wandered a long way from its radical roots – when it was a church that was in the forefront of standing up for people and reaching across the religious divide. I have been disappointed by the lack of grace that we've shown to others. It's been easier to just keep preaching that you must be born again. I utterly accept that you must be born again, but what does that look like in terms of how I treat my neighbour?

Isobel pointed to the suspension of the Northern Ireland Assembly and the lack of political leadership as 'an opportunity' for the churches 'to make a distinctive contribution' to dealing with the past, rooted in a Christian perspective on forgiveness.

> Ultimately, forgiveness isn't an option for Christians. If you go back to the Lord's Prayer, we are called to forgive no matter how hard that is. We are called to forgive even though you've been the victim of injustice and even though those who have done you this injustice are not repenting, or don't even perceive they have done you an injustice. I have the responsibility before God of doing what he commands me to do, which is to forgive. That's easy to say but incredibly difficult to do.

'We have let the Lord down.'

Joe Campbell has been part of First Holywood in Co. Down, pretty much his entire life. He has been an elder for four decades and has served as the congregation's clerk of session.

Joe's maternal grandparents were a mixed marriage and this family background predisposed him to reach across the traditional divide. As a young man, he worked with the YMCA and Scripture Union. 'In the YMCA during the late 1970s, 1980s we were open six nights a week in the centre of Belfast for teenagers at a time when there wasn't much happening in the city at night. Often, especially in winter, we were the only light on after six o'clock.' The programme attracted 'hundreds' of young people, Catholic and Protestant. 'It was terrific, groundbreaking, cross-community work in the neutral city centre when segregation in housing provided no opportunity for young teenagers to meet. The team of volunteer leaders were both Catholic and Protestant. We trained, worshipped and worked together, and occasionally had communion together.'

Congregational life in those days was seen as a safe haven away from the increasing political violence. Few were interested in cross-community work.

> With one or two exceptions, people in my congregation weren't interested in front line youth work. They never asked about the cross-community dimensions or the stress of working with Belfast's teenagers. There may have been a bomb somewhere on Saturday night and people killed. Sunday morning worship, it often wasn't mentioned. It was as if we were worshipping in another country. I remember showing a fine evangelical couple around the YMCA and explaining some of the work with young people. One of them said to me, 'But what happens if these Protestant young men get attached to a Catholic girl?'

Joe was part of a network that helped young people who had fallen foul of paramilitaries escape to safety, usually to Scotland.

You'd get a phone call from a boy's mother or a youth worker. Drive into Belfast and find that young fella hiding in the loft of a terrace house and get him down into the car and away. Sometimes we'd bring them to our house, or they would sleep in a tent in our garden till the next day or the day after till they could get out to safety.

After eleven years in this work, 'I was exhausted almost to breaking point.' He and his family were offered a year-long sabbatical at the Mennonite Biblical Seminary in Elkhart, Indiana, USA. The Mennonites are Christians of the radical Anabaptist tradition that emerged during the Reformation. Mennonites were the first to advocate the separation of church and state and adult baptism. They are also pacifists. Joe first encountered them through Joe Liechty, a Mennonite based at the Irish School of Ecumenics. 'Mennonites understood peace work from their long pacifist tradition. I felt affirmed, understood, and encouraged by them.'

At Elkhart, Joe participated in the local community's victim–offender mediation programmes, gleaning insights he would later apply in Northern Ireland. He was inspired by Mennonite peace theology, discovering that the Bible had a lot to say about war, violence and peacebuilding.

It's a principled peace stance Mennonites take. I also began to see the weaknesses in our 'just war' theory in PCI and most other Christian denominations. Mennonites are also very strong on community. It is much more than an hour of worship on a Sunday morning, it is helping one another live out the faith in a pretty hostile world. We don't have a coherent peace theology in PCI, but our Coleraine Declaration developed at a special residential General Assembly in 1990 is certainly a challenge to the traditional views of violence and war.

When Joe returned, he was part of a local inter-church group in Holywood. People met in each other's churches, learnt about that tradition, and prayed together. 'But in those days, it would never have appeared in the church bulletin nor been promoted or particularly encouraged.'

Joe helped establish Mediation Northern Ireland, which he later joined as staff (1995–2006). He also helped PCI set up an internal conciliation service for intra-congregational conflicts. 'Mediation Northern Ireland supported and helped staff the work of the Parades Commission during the very tense early years of its work. We were also involved in cultural awareness training for new RUC [Royal Ulster Constabulary] officers as well as supporting the change management process after the Patten Report on policing.' All of this work carried its own risk for civilian peace workers. 'Some had security on our houses and cars. Those were the times of undercar booby trap bombs. Some days we might have been working with senior police in the morning and in the afternoon or evening with republicans or loyalists. You knew there was a risk but you aimed to be wise, sensible and to trust God.'

Between 2006 and 2010 Joe and his wife Janet were PCI overseas workers in Nepal. 'I wasn't going to do evangelism or church planting. I was supporting peacebuilding efforts after the ten-year war. PCI was very happy to send me in that context. Thirty years ago, I'm not sure the church would send somebody overseas to do peace work. Things have changed. We have come a long way.'

But while 'things have changed', Joe believes PCI still has some way to go.

> We need to display much more humility. We could have been more active in peace work much earlier, less chaplain to one side, and more intent on listening and acting on behalf of both sides. We have let the Lord down and we have not supported our people the way we could have and should have. Hindsight is a great thing, but it seems as if we put the harmony of PCI before the good of society. The holding of the church together at the lowest common denominator was more important than following the prince of peace into uncharted waters. The church should be at the front line of proclaiming the core truths of the Gospel: forgiveness, loving enemies, turning the other cheek and going the extra mile. The hard sayings of Jesus which too often we think are only applicable to other people. I like to think we would do it better next time, but I hope and pray we never have to again.

'There was an appetite in the Christian evangelical population to do something about the country.'

David Hewitt grew up in a Brethren congregation. At university, he was drawn to the Presbyterian Church through the ministry of Welshman Rev. J. Glyn Owen (1919–2017) at Berry Street in Belfast. 'He attracted many students of our day. I didn't join to become a Presbyterian – I joined because Glyn Owen was a greatly gifted teacher of scripture.' He met his future wife Margaret there. After their marriage, they joined First Holywood. David served as an elder, clerk of session, and led a Bible class for teenagers.

David was a solicitor and also played international rugby. 'Rugby was good because it was all-island, so you were playing with guys from the four provinces.' He was in his early thirties when the Troubles began. A chance meeting with a Catholic solicitor sparked his interest in peacemaking. 'I was in Chichester Street one day when the Troubles were quite hot, and I ran into Terry Donaghy (1934–2009) and he says, "David, this is awful. What are we going to do?"' They created the Northern Consensus Group (1984–96), a small group of professionals concerned about the Troubles. They produced discussion documents that reached governments in Dublin and Belfast, and spoke with government ministers. 'We wanted to represent both sides from a rational and Christian point of view because we were all committed believers in Jesus Christ, Protestant and Catholic. We found that we got a good hearing, particularly when we prefaced any meeting we had with them with discussion documents.'

David was one of the founders of ECONI in 1985. ECONI is regarded as among Northern Ireland's most effective faith-based peacemaking organisations.[16] During our interview, David produced many of the Northern Consensus Group's and ECONI's printed resources. ECONI's first publication was a booklet called 'For God and His Glory Alone', a Biblical case for peacemaking that challenged the religious–nationalist sentiment behind the popular slogan 'For God and Ulster'. David recalled collecting the first copies of the booklet at the printer's.

'I was going down James Street and from the other end came Fr Gerry Reynolds from Clonard Monastery on his bike. He said, "David, where's the book? Where's the book?" Gerry Reynolds ended up with the first copy of "For God and His Glory Alone" and he was thrilled.' ECONI developed an ambitious programme of education and activism. 'ECONI grew because there was an appetite in the Christian evangelical population to do something about the country.'

David confided in Presbyterian ministers who were engaged in similar work.

> John Dunlop, Godfrey Brown, Ken Newell would all have been close friends of mine. They would always have been helpful, advising me on what they thought should be done. My experience in the denomination as a whole was pretty limited because I was too busy with other things. But I never had any cause to want to move from being a Presbyterian.

Later, David served on the Parades Commission, which mediated disputes between the Orange Order and residents' groups. Within his congregation, 'There were a few who were quite *orange* Orangemen, who would not have been happy about my role. But the majority would have accepted it. There were gentlemanly Orangemen in the congregation who were very supportive of me at a personal level, which I shall be always grateful for.' His own stereotypes about intransigent Orangemen were challenged. 'I learnt a lot, not just about the politics of the province. Prejudice that I had against the Orange would have softened when I got to know some of them.'

'PCI weren't prepared to pay for [peacemaking].'

As a child, Laura Coulter was sent to Knock Presbyterian in East Belfast. At twelve, she became a Christian at a Scripture Union camp. At eighteen, she participated in a Campus Crusade for Christ summer scheme in Cork, where she lived with Catholic women – her first experience encountering people from the Catholic community. While Laura would have been unsure on the question of whether Catholics were really Christians, she found real faith among those she met. 'They would have taken me to the charismatic prayer meeting, and then we would have gone to a nightclub afterwards. That was total culture shock! I spent hours talking to them about what they believed. I found out that what we had in common was the important stuff. I've never been the same since.'

After university, Laura volunteered for a year at the Christian Renewal Centre (CRC) in Rostrevor, Co. Down, a charismatic and ecumenical community headed by Church of Ireland Rev. Cecil Kerr. 'It was the height of the Troubles, so in some ways it was quite radical. I saw Catholics and Protestants come together and I thought this is the way it should be.' During her volunteer year, Presbyterian Rev. David Armstrong (Chapter 2) spent some time there. 'Seeing what he'd been through brought home to me how intolerant our society is.'

Early in her career, Laura worked in community development. This included a stint in the 174 Trust, based in a Presbyterian congregation in a Catholic-nationalist-republican part of the city (Chapter 2). She managed its café and trained young men as catering staff as part of a government employment scheme. The café was the target of vandalism and break-ins. 'I wouldn't have been there if

I wasn't a Christian. I was at risk at times.' Like the locals, she was harassed by the British Army. 'The soldiers had a checkpoint and used to throw eggs when you walked past. The staff would come in with egg all over them. The antagonism with the army was something I never experienced before, coming from leafy East Belfast.' The locals looked after her, especially if she had to lock up after dark. 'They wouldn't have left me on my own.' Years later, Laura worked on the Parades Commission, a body set up to mediate disputes between the Orange Order and residents' groups.

These experiences made Laura an uneasy fit in her congregation. 'People from my own church told me I shouldn't have been doing what I was doing.' After living in other parts of Northern Ireland, Laura returned to Belfast and began attending Knock again. At that time, the associate minister, Rev. David Montgomery, encouraged her to become the congregation's peace agent. She helped establish Knock's peace group, which is still running. Laura also facilitated a study group with a Catholic parish which explored issues of faith and politics. When Laura moved to Kirkpatrick Memorial in East Belfast, she established a small peace committee and supported the congregation's peace agent. The congregation's leadership adopted and passed the 'unity pilgrims' model. The 'unity pilgrims' were originally developed by Fr Gerry Reynolds from Clonard Monastery as a structured way for people from a parish or congregation to visit churches from another tradition.[17] 'We identified four local churches, including the Catholic Church, and once a month we would visit one church as representatives of Kirkpatrick Memorial.'

Between 2006 and 2009, Laura was employed by PCI as a Peacemaking Officer on its Peacemaking

Programme, which was funded by the International Fund for Ireland. Debs Irwin ran the accompanying 'Preparing Youth for Peace' programme. Laura's role was to support peace agents through regional gatherings and an annual conference. She also helped co-ordinate a team of PCI conciliators, which is still in operation. She wrote a five-week 'Gospel in Conflict' training course for use in congregations, with an accompanying DVD. 'That has now disappeared somewhere – nobody knows where it is. I've got one copy, which is probably the only one left!' At the time, PCI made a deliberate decision not to use the word 'reconciliation' in its Peacemaking Programme. 'Some people are suspicious of reconciliation. I had people phone me up – they were nervous about meeting people from the Catholic Church. If people had theological problems with the Catholic Church, it was too much to say we're going to be reconciling with your Catholic brothers and sisters.' The term 'good relations' was used instead.

With funding due to run out, PCI's General Assembly debated whether the church should continue the programme. 'We sat in the General Assembly and listened to the debate. But the motion was not carried. PCI weren't prepared to pay for it. We were really devastated. We thought, "This is what the Presbyterian Church thinks of building peace." That was very disappointing because we felt we were beginning to make in-roads and develop peacemaking within the denomination.' Within weeks, Laura's employment had ended. Some congregations retained peace agents and peace groups. But within a few years, the centrally organised conferences and other development activities had ceased, unable to be carried out entirely by volunteers.

Between 2013 and 2014 Laura was one of six regional development officers employed by the Irish Churches Peace Project (ICPP), an initiative of PCI, the Catholic Church, the Church of Ireland, the Methodist Church and the Irish Council of Churches. It was funded by the EU and government departments in Northern Ireland and the Republic. Like PCI's Peacemaking Programme, Laura felt it was only just beginning to make progress when funding ended. Before it ended, Laura left her post to work on a peacebuilding team within the United Mission to Nepal. She asked, 'Why did the churches not continue that programme? If there had been more strategic thinking, we could have planned to continue it. We need something like that for ten years or more to make an impact in terms of community engagement and peacebuilding.'

'Perhaps if the church had put a greater value on women in leadership, we would have been a more reconciled church.'

Heather's family attended a rural congregation.

Once every year our minister used to preach a fiery sermon that if anyone in the church cared about Jesus, they should come forward. But this was a country congregation, and nobody moved from their seats. Ever. One year, my sisters and I decided we wanted to do something. We went round after church and met him at the front of the manse and said: 'We're coming in response to your sermon.' He said: 'Oh, I didn't mean you. I meant the men.' That was fifty years ago, and we accepted it then. I don't accept now that women are not an important part of the church.

Heather became enthused about her faith at university, which inspired her to volunteer in Africa. There, she was impressed by the witness of Irish nuns. 'They were dressed in these habits and looked so out of place. Yet they spent forty to fifty years in the one place, serving the people. They were committed to prayer and lived a very joyful life.'

When Heather returned to Northern Ireland, she sought a congregation that was reaching out to Catholics. 'We started off with shared Bible studies. We would read a Bible passage, hear a few thoughts from the readers and share what it meant to us. Catholics ministered to me. My faith was deepened by the depth of the prayers in the Catholic tradition.' She also has been part of an inter-church women's group. 'I feel in fellowship with my Catholic friends. We don't even think in terms of Catholic/Protestant. We're just a group of women praying.'

Heather's minister invited Catholics to pray and read the Bible during Presbyterian services. 'At first some of the session [of elders] said we should vet the Catholic prayer. Now Catholics are invited to speak freely from the front.' Some families left the congregation. 'There was a lot of fear in the church. Fear of being censured by groups within the church and without; worry that we would be letting victims down if we engaged with the Catholic Church.' Heather was always interested in the first media interview with a new Moderator as he began his year of office. 'He would be asked: "Would you join in worship with Catholics?" Sometimes he would say, "No." I felt that wasn't very welcoming. Often it meant he wouldn't engage in any meaningful way or try to build bridges.'

Heather was a peace agent and attended PCI's annual peace conferences. 'I found it a very helpful meeting and was inspired by what people were doing in other congregations. But then the external funding was cut, and PCI didn't value it enough to continue funding. It's such a loss. Reconciliation shouldn't just be part of mission, it should be mainstream – central to our Gospel witness.'

Heather attended PCI's annual General Assembly and was disappointed with the way difficult conversations were conducted. She felt communication between congregations and the denominational bureaucracy in Church House could be improved. 'You feel let down if Church House is saying something you don't agree with and there's no easy means of dialogue.' She also felt PCI had not recognised the powerful peacemaking witness of its female ministers and members.

> Lesley Carroll, Liz Hughes, Ruth Patterson, Cheryl Meban, and Anne Toland – they have managed to make it into ministry but there's a glass ceiling. None of them was ever made Moderator or Clerk of the Assembly. None has been spokeswoman for the church in any meaningful way. Yet all these women have been extraordinarily committed to reconciliation. Perhaps if the church had put a greater value on women in leadership, we would have been a more reconciled church.

'This was more than a job; this was a calling.'

Trevor Reaney has been Clerk and Chief Executive of the Northern Ireland Assembly (2008–16), Chief Executive of the Northern Ireland Policing Board (2004–8), and Chief Executive of Craigavon Borough Council (1996–2003). He has been an elder in three congregations in different parts of Northern Ireland. 'As I got to Chief Executive level, it became more than running an organisation. It was also about providing civic leadership and taking risks. That was very much about trying to make a difference from a Christian perspective.'

Trevor was raised Presbyterian and spent most of his childhood in West Presbyterian in Ballymena, a relatively peaceful area. 'The Troubles were something we saw on TV.' When he moved to Armagh and then to work for Craigavon Borough Council, the Troubles came closer to home. He contended with the Drumcree disputes, a bomb explosion in Portadown town centre, and the murder of a council employee, Adrian Lamph. Adrian was working in a civic amenity site when a loyalist paramilitary rode up on a bicycle and shot him in the head. The attack was purely sectarian. 'I supported the mayor in providing civic leadership, primarily in preventing retaliation. We decided to lower all the council flags to half-mast for a few days, to show support for a Catholic employee in a largely Protestant workforce in a largely Protestant town.'

Trevor's time on the Policing Board included implementing the Patten Report, which resulted in the creation of the new Police Service of Northern Ireland. 'The reforms were very controversial amongst the Protestant community. It was a challenge to keep Protestant politicians, Catholic politicians and independent members from both sides of the community on board.' In his work with the Assembly, 'I tried to bring a Christian influence of decency – being impartial, unbiased, and providing politicians with good research, advice and guidance on procedure. I wanted to help people treat others as they wanted to be treated themselves.' Others also worked hard to make a difference. 'Christian folk in public service have

given a lot of themselves, taking a heavy burden. They
didn't take the easy approach to life: this was more than
a job; this was a calling. We believed we could make a
difference for God by taking an opportunity to influence
for good.'

Trevor's work was stressful.

> My wife, Liz, has been very supportive with
> encouragement and prayer as we have tried to live
> through the difficult times. We have been blessed
> with ministers who have been good at providing
> pastoral support. We've had other members of our
> congregations who have understood the nature of
> the role and have been supportive in prayer and
> friendship. With the level of stress and demand,
> church was a place where you were able to get your
> batteries recharged.

Trevor regretted that PCI didn't speak out as much as
he thought it should have done, especially in difficult
times like Drumcree. 'The General Assembly could have
done more to help local ministers put out messages that
were exhorting people to behave in a particular way,
encouraging people in response to a terrorist incident or
in the political process.' He wants churches to focus more
on forgiveness. 'I never experienced the loss of a loved
one in the Troubles. So, it might be easier for me to say
forgiveness needs more emphasis. But holding bitterness
and un-forgiveness can be very damaging. Forgiveness
doesn't always require repentance from the other party.'
He has a distinct view on reconciliation, because to him
it implies restoring a relationship that was already there.
'Growing up in Ballymena, I lived amongst Protestants

primarily, Presbyterians often. I didn't have a relationship with Roman Catholic people that was then fractured, so I had nothing to be reconciled. Reconciliation is not something I think a lot about. Rather, I think about building relationships for the first time.'

'We're here, and we're staying.'

Cynthia ran a shop in a mixed border town during the worst decades of the Troubles. 'Everyone coming in the door was treated with respect. Most people are not going to do any harm.'

Cynthia's husband was a farmer and had been in the police reserves. After their third child, she begged him to leave the security forces. 'A lot of people were murdered quite close to where I live. It was very frightening. I thought, how can I cope if he is murdered?' She witnessed a neighbour, an Ulster Defence Regiment (UDR) man, shot dead at his front door. 'There were times when I said, "I'm not staying here." But my husband said, "Look, everyone can't go." It was a case of saying, "We're here, and we're staying."'

Cynthia recalled a gun battle in the street outside the shop. 'We couldn't come out. It took a wee while for that to pass over. But we were resilient and the people who came were good people. There was never animosity and you never felt intimidated.'

Cynthia's determination to get on with her work was rooted in her faith. 'God created this world, and it's up to us to look after it. We are meant to be workers and we're meant to get on. My attitude is, you keep going and make it better because if you don't, things slip and get worse. We trusted God to keep us safe.'

Though she had never met him, Cynthia was inspired by former Moderator Rev. John Dunlop, whose example encouraged her to keep going. Presbyterian ministers in the town came and went over the years. She was heartened by one who was particularly good at building relationships across the whole community. She also believed Christian women had played an important part in holding society together. 'Maybe I'm prejudiced, but I think women were great in church life.'

Cynthia believed people and politicians should be striving for reconciliation. 'You have to mix, no matter what.' She said some victims feel forgotten, and the church should speak out for them. 'You can't forget the past, but you have to think of the future. We're all going to have to face judgment. If we can't leave this world a better place, we haven't done anything. If you can't show God's love – what have you left?'

'We used to keep records in the school of the
pupils that had been killed in the Troubles.'

Gregory worked as a schoolteacher near a violent inner-city interface.

We used to keep records in the school of the pupils that had been killed in the Troubles. We stopped because the figures were just horrendous. Pupils would have been taken out of school because something had happened to their parents. Then there were other ones who would have been sucked into rioting and hijacking. Some would come very sleepy into school, a bit dishevelled. There might have been rioting in their district and their house would be right in the middle of it.

Gregory lived in the area before he married.

> Travelling across the city was fraught. Once when a
> bomb blew up, I was blown off my motorbike. I lay
> there, and the army picked me up. I got back on
> the bike and drove off. Other times I got stopped by
> masked people. They'd surround you and take your
> helmet off. Then they'd say, 'Yeah, we know you from
> school.' I always wondered what happened if they
> didn't know you.

In such circumstances, pupils struggled to reach their
potential. 'Even just to get to school and home on
time was an achievement.' Gregory helped set up cross-
community schools projects bringing children together
in the local area, including trips to the Republic and
England. There had been cross-community schemes
running for some time which took children to the
United States. Because Gregory's projects were closer
to home, they could afford to involve more children.
He worked closely with Catholic teachers whose efforts
he described as beyond the call of duty. The children
took several trips per year, which included activities like
singing, poetry and sport.

> Once, two brand new girls who had never been in
> the project came in – a wee girl from a Catholic
> school and a wee girl from a Protestant school. They
> sat down beside each other and were laughing. They
> said, 'We know each other.' Their houses backed onto
> the peace wall and they could look into each other's
> gardens. They had watched each other growing up,
> but never met. They swapped phone numbers.

Gregory believed the programmes opened children up to new perspectives and gave them confidence to become good citizens. Today, he is gratified when he sees former pupils working hard and contributing to the community.

In this part of the city, the churches offered support in difficult times. 'The churches couldn't help but be involved because they were in the middle of it. All the different churches welcomed people into their church halls whenever there was bombs and people were put out of their houses.' On one occasion, sisters were forced out of their home a few days before they were due to go on a trip. 'The mother brought them up with their cases and all. She said, "They're safer with you. They'll have a bed. Right now they're sleeping in a church hall."' But Gregory felt that outside the most violent areas, the churches didn't respond to the Troubles. 'It was basically a working-class Troubles. Everywhere else, the church was out of it. Some churches went on as if life was no different.'

Gregory believed churches, politicians and the community had not grasped that 'it was going to be so much harder to build the peace than it was to stop the war'. During the Troubles,

> People could see the advantage of getting the kids together. As soon as the Good Friday Agreement, I said, 'Who is going to keep getting the kids together now?' There are young boys being recruited to paramilitary organisations at this minute and they weren't alive during the Troubles. You really must continue to make a big effort, like we did. In regard to the church, this is the time when the hard work should start.

'I just think the future can be different.'

Trevor Ringland is a solicitor and former rugby international. He has been a politician in the Ulster Unionist Party and the Northern Ireland Conservatives. His father was in the RUC and served in different parts of Northern Ireland, where the family attended Methodist and Presbyterian congregations. When Trevor married a Presbyterian, he joined her congregation, Knock in East Belfast.

Growing up in a police family showed Trevor 'the consequences of hatred and conflict'. Once, his father was trapped for hours inside a police station after an Irish Republican Army (IRA) gun attack. The family didn't know whether he was dead or alive. At the same time, police houses were being attacked by loyalist paramilitaries in his hometown. He recalled his father dealing with distraught families. But rugby convinced him there could be genuine friendships across religious and political divides. 'In rugby, there was an Irishness that could be comfortably British and a Britishness that was comfortably Irish. Rugby has something that gets it right on this island, where others got it so wrong.'

In 1996, Trevor, together with his friend Hugo Mac Neill and the support of Irish Rugby, helped organise a 'Peace International' rugby match between Ireland and the Barbarians in Dublin. 'Over 30,000 people turned up at Lansdowne Road to say we wanted peace,' Trevor said. Victims of the Troubles were invited onto the pitch before the match. 'When you met those lovely people, you just asked yourself, how can we make sure this does not happen again?' The media interviewed Trevor after the match, but 'I was reluctant to give answers because I felt I didn't know enough.' That experience led him to 'find out more'. He engaged with all aspects of society, including those of the Protestant tradition that he had little real understanding of, like the Orange Order. He met Presbyterian Rev. William Bingham, who negotiated on behalf of the Orange Order during the Drumcree disputes of the late 1990s. In 1998, after the three Quinn boys were killed in an attack linked to Drumcree, Bingham urged Orangemen to go home with the words, 'no road is worth a life' (Chapter 2). 'At a time when our country could have descended into real conflict, he showed leadership. I also gained respect for him in the way he looked to try and find solutions to problems. His faith and his adherence to the Christian message impacted me then and has done ever since.'

Trevor has promoted grassroots peacemaking initiatives over the years: the One Small Step Campaign, which encourages people to reconcile in everyday ways in their local communities; Peaceplayers International, which brings children from divided communities together through sport; and Game of Three Halves, where children from different backgrounds come together on integrated teams to play rugby, football and Gaelic. With even sport divided on political/religious lines, this programme gives children a chance to play sports that they would not have had before. These civic and sporting initiatives were often supported by local congregations. In fact, Game of Three Halves was a 'small step' pioneered by a youth worker in Knock Presbyterian, Paul Brown.

Trevor said, 'The church has always been a source of support. I always find the ministers that I've been involved with have been prepared to talk, to listen, to give advice.' He acknowledged there was disagreement within PCI on a range of issues, not least of which was the priority that should be given to peacemaking. He hoped PCI would place peacemaking at the core of its mission rather than seeing it as an 'add on'. He said,

> The strength and the challenge of the Presbyterian Church is its diversity. That diversity encourages debate. If there is debate, you probably have a better chance of getting things right. Things take a bit longer to move in a direction that you favour than you might like. But sometimes that's not a bad thing, to give people time to come to terms with changes that need to be made.

Trevor said his generation has had to make 'hard decisions', like allowing former paramilitaries to hold political office. 'We've been doing that, so the future generations don't make the same mistakes we did. What worries me is that we will squander the hard decisions that we have taken.' Yet he is encouraged by the grace that has been shown by people from all backgrounds.

> There have been people that showed a level of forgiveness a lot of people couldn't be capable of. Then there are people who have taken a pragmatic approach to forgiveness, recognising that the individuals who they need to forgive are not looking for forgiveness. Grace has been shown by an awful lot of people who've stayed quiet, even though there's an anger underneath the surface. They are all our heroes. That's created a space for our society to move beyond conflict.

He remained hopeful. 'I just think the future can be different and we should not squander the opportunity we currently have to ensure it is one that is peaceful and prosperous for the benefit of us all.'

'Who are the keepers of the story of the common good within Presbyterianism?'

Lynda Gould was baptised and brought up in Knock Presbyterian in East Belfast. She has remained in the congregation all her life and was serving as clerk of session at the time of our interview. Lynda was in her thirties when she discovered her mother was raised Catholic.

> After my uncle died, my aunt rediscovered her faith and started wearing a crucifix. And we were like, 'What's going on'? This was when I discovered that my mum's family were not Presbyterian. It suddenly made sense why she never fully joined our church and why she brought us up to be mindful of all people as human beings as opposed to putting labels on them.

As a teenager, Lynda had a conversion experience at a youth mission. 'Back then, I would have understood it as the need for salvation. I don't use that language now. But it made sense and I was very unquestioning.' Shortly after, Lynda was assaulted on her way to help at a church event.

> There were two responses from other Christians. There were people who said an awful thing has happened. Then there were those who quoted the Bible verse, 'all things work together for good for those who love God'. Even at that early age, I thought, 'I don't think so.' I can't accept that interpretation of scripture in terms of an awful thing happening to me.

I realised then that scripture could be used to gloss over hard things rather than confront something that just wasn't right.

The Troubles first touched Lynda directly in 1979, when a member of her youth group was murdered. John Donaldson, a solicitor, was shot dead after leaving a police station in West Belfast, where he had delivered a summons. Her youth leaders brought her group to visit a Catholic Church near where the incident occurred. 'That was the first time I'd ever travelled into that part of Belfast.' This incident, and her youth leaders' response, sparked Lynda's interest in peacemaking. Her youth group also visited the Church of the Resurrection at Queen's University, where Church of Ireland Rev. Cecil Kerr was chaplain. They met evangelical Catholics through Kerr's ecumenical ministry.

When her congregation established a peace group in the early 1990s, Lynda joined. Over the years, the group has organised an annual Peace Sunday, hustings with politicians prior to elections, and activities with other local congregations. Yet in a congregation of around 1,000 families, only a handful of people have been involved with the peace group at any one time. 'Knock does what every Presbyterian church does: set up a group. The moment you do that, you marginalise it. It becomes, "Oh, that's what those people there do." We always struggled to make peacemaking mainstream.'

Lynda worked for several faith-based and secular community organisations over the years, including eight years as a trainer and facilitator for ECONI. As noted above, ECONI was one of Northern Ireland's most effective faith-based peacemaking organisations. ECONI grounded its case for peacemaking in the Bible, which was crucial for changing the hearts and minds of evangelicals. 'You can say whatever you want to evangelicals, but it won't be heard unless you can unpack it from scripture. I still meet people who participated in ECONI and they talk about it in the sense that through what we did, something happened that matters.'

Lynda appreciated the witness of those who had been voices for peace and other social causes over the years. But overall, 'The way we describe the Gospel is too small. It's all about atonement and redemption, in the sense of personal salvation. Then you don't know how to fit peacebuilding into that. It's an add-on, as opposed to being fundamental to the Gospel.' She also wondered, 'Who are the keepers of the story of the common good within Presbyterianism? All our stories are about private salvation. There would be Presbyterians who would live the common good, but they're the people who often don't turn up at General Assembly.'

Lynda believed PCI had reverted to 'survival' mode, trying to cling onto members. 'I'm not optimistic about PCI being great game changers. But you do see folks who are really committed to doing something on the ground. I'm more hopeful for a grassroots movement for change.'

'PCI certainly became far more conservative and right wing than it had ever been before.'

Lillian and Roger lived in different parts of Northern Ireland during the Troubles. Their current congregation is in a mixed town. Lillian has been the congregation's peace agent; and part of an inter-church group and inter-church women's group. Roger's church involvement has been sporadic. At the time of the interview, he had stopped attending.

> A certain Presbyterian clergyman made scurrilous remarks about Catholics during the protest at Twaddell.[18] I expected someone within the Presbyterian Church would throw their arms up in horror. But I didn't spot that and I stopped going to church again after that, despite the fact that the clergyman we have in our congregation is an A-1 man.

Lillian grew up in a predominantly Protestant area and was in secondary school when the Troubles started. It seemed as if her congregation and her community didn't respond at all.

> Looking back on it now, it was as if we were in a bubble. You listened to the news bulletins alright, but it was seen as not to do with you. If something appalling had happened there maybe would have been prayers in church. But apart from that, no discussion. There still doesn't seem to be a recognition that the people who are perceived to have started the Troubles were not aliens who had come from outer space. They were part of this society who felt they had not been listened to.

Lillian was disappointed that PCI 'circled the wagons' rather than reaching out to others, attributing this to fear of Rev. Ian Paisley.

> Paisley set up his church and was drawing people to it. When I was young and for a long time before that,

the Presbyterian Church had been known for being liberal and radical. It pioneered things like the rights of tenants to own their land. PCI certainly became far more conservative and right wing than it had ever been before and the radical liberals were forgotten about.

Roger believed the town's sporting and civic associations had been better at building relationships than the churches. 'It never struck me that the Presbyterian Church were doing anything or not doing anything. I didn't notice any influence on the community. Maybe they withdrew.' He also thought the Orange Order had prevented PCI from reaching out. 'The elephant in the room is the Orange Order. I've loads of friends who are Orangemen but they want what I would call at best a benign apartheid. It's anti-Catholicism, it's near enough anti-anybody that doesn't agree with them. So, they'd be anti-me as well.'

They were heartened that when their congregation's current minister came in the late 1990s, he prioritised inter-church activities. 'He'd have more contact with the Catholic clergy than the Protestant clergy,' Roger said approvingly. Lillian added, 'His predecessor sat in our house once and said, "I don't know any Catholics living in this town."' When Lillian became the congregation's peace agent, she attended regional conferences organised by PCI. 'There hadn't been a conference for two years and I emailed to find out why. They emailed back that they didn't think the Peacemaking Programme was terribly effective. I could see that it maybe wasn't. A lot of the congregations never bothered themselves to appoint peace agents or peace groups. They weren't really interested.'

Both fear PCI is retreating into a conservatism that is harming all aspects of its witness. Lillian said,

> During the Troubles, PCI became conservative in every way. In the 1970s, PCI voted at the General Assembly to agree the ordination of women clergy. Then they put in a conscience clause which meant that it was okay to ordain women clergy, but you didn't have to have them in your pulpit if you felt in your conscience that it wasn't appropriate. I think that's shocking. What's more, there are fears among women clergy and women elders that there could be a move to rescind women's ordination.

Lillian saw some progress in her local inter-church groups.

> The women's cross-community group started off gingerly enough. At first it was more social than anything. Then we started doing Bible studies together. One of the last books that we worked on was by [Presbyterian] Rev Ruth Patterson (Chapter 2). So, we've got to that stage where we can actually deal in faith issues. But the difficulty is that I feel you're not reaching out to the right people. The folk in the cross-community group would never have been extreme in their political views anyway.

'What we have here is a progression rather than reconciliation.'

Fiona and Grant belong to a small congregation in a border county in the Republic. Fiona was raised Catholic but became Presbyterian when they married. 'The Presbyterian Church was simpler and much more democratic. I know some Presbyterians wouldn't consider Catholics to be Christians. But I've always thought I was a Christian.' There was some opposition from their families. Grant said, 'When we married thirty-odd years ago it was a mixed marriage. It wouldn't be regarded like that now.'

Even though there was intense violence nearby on the other side of the border, the Troubles did not impinge much on their lives. Grant said, 'We were at peace here. But whenever you went across the border, you had to go through an army checkpoint and there was high security.' The Troubles were rarely spoken about in their congregation. Fiona said, 'Sometimes I thought we prayed for other places in the world rather than Northern Ireland. It's only latterly that we'd pray for Northern Ireland – sometimes I thought our response was a bit lacking.' Neither could think of anything PCI had done to respond to the Troubles.

The lack of violence made relationships with their Catholic neighbours more 'easy-going'. Fiona said, 'In the north they've experienced worse things. They have their reasons for never integrating. There has been separation of areas for safety reasons and I don't think that has changed.' They were positive about Presbyterians' relationships in their community. But when someone suggested the congregation put a plaque on the wall to honour a former member who had been prominent in Ulster-Scots culture, they decided against it. Grant said, 'We thought maybe we'd be drawing attention to ourselves. Maybe some of the bad boys in the area would see it up on our wall and vandalise the place.' Fiona added, 'We have good relationships within the community and didn't want to alienate ourselves.'

Over the years, almost all the congregation's ministers have been from Northern Ireland. People in the congregation identified as Irish and Presbyterian, but this was not the case for their ministers. Grant, who served as an elder and clerk of session, said this made the congregation careful when calling a minister. They wanted to be sure their minister would work alongside the local priest and in community organisations, so they asked a question about this in their interviews with prospective candidates.

Fiona and Grant were involved in some of the peace initiatives in border areas after the Belfast Agreement. Fiona said, 'There's been funding for a local resource centre where people have had more opportunities to mix. It has brought people together more. We didn't have a big split before, but probably we mixed during the week and went our own way on a Sunday. The churches didn't integrate. Now we would have many more joint services, ecumenical services.' They weren't sure if more inter-church activities would have evolved anyway. 'It's easier for us because we don't have the baggage or the bad experiences. What we have here is a progression rather than reconciliation.'

'This is a good thing and the Lord will protect us.'

Amanda grew up in the Republic in the 1950s. 'The Protestant population was small, and we got on exceedingly well. We had next-door neighbours who were Catholic. The relationships were very good, but there was a slight feeling of, "I don't want my child to marry a Catholic." There was very little social mixing.' From a young age, Amanda wanted a career where she could help people. She was inspired by her parents. 'They were sympathetic and believed in doing what was right.' They invited

Travellers into their home. 'They came into the kitchen and were given cups of tea and a bit of bread.' Another formative childhood occasion came when Amanda was visiting a friend in Dublin. They found a man lying on the street drunk. 'He was sufficiently able to say where he lived, and we took him home. I remember thinking at the time: This is awful. What can we do about this?'

When she was a teenager, Amanda's family moved to Northern Ireland. The Troubles started around the time she finished university. Newly married and living in a predominantly Protestant town, the violence did not impinge much on her life. She worked abroad for a few years, where she became friends with a Catholic. 'I learned that he might believe something slightly different from me, but that should not affect relationships. When we came home, that's what got us thinking we have got to do something. Making peace is part of being a Christian.' She became more convinced of this over time. 'I felt very strongly that this was the right thing to do. I felt this is a good thing and the Lord will protect us. You can't let the IRA win. They've got to see that people are serious about making peace and that we are not going to be put off.'

Amanda became part of a congregation that had a partnership with a Catholic church. She estimated that during the Troubles, only 'about ten' Presbyterian congregations partnered with Catholic churches – a tiny number considering PCI had well over 500 congregations. Some families left her congregation when it became clear it was committed to peacemaking. 'But as people left, others joined. Many of them joined because they felt the church was moving forward and they wanted to be part of that. I have real sympathy for the people who had been there quite some time and were a bit shaken by what was happening but didn't move. That was courageous.'

Amanda believed PCI did not support congregations that were taking risks for peace. 'The church made statements, but they didn't go anywhere. They could have got clergy together, got someone like John Dunlop or Ken Newell to chat with them to talk about what was happening so they wouldn't be afraid.' She was inspired by her congregation's long-term commitment. 'The big lesson is that it can actually succeed. You're not going to be annihilated. Nothing awful is going to happen if you bring a Catholic church together with a Protestant church. But it takes time and you must have a plan. It takes at least ten years to change an organisation.'

Her own experiences have convinced her reconciliation is possible. 'For me, reconciliation expresses what's actually happening. You're coming together with people who think differently. Reconciliation is understanding the needs of the other person almost as well as you understand your own and working at that level.'

CHAPTER 8

Politicians

Many Presbyterians held political office during the Troubles, primarily for Northern Ireland's two main unionist parties: the Ulster Unionist Party (UUP), the largest party until 2004; and the Democratic Unionist Party (DUP), which was founded by Rev. Ian Paisley and is now the largest party. Presbyterians were also prominent in the smaller, cross-community Alliance Party. We spoke with five politicians, who between them served at all levels of government: local councillors, Members of the Northern Ireland Legislative Assembly (MLAs), and Westminster MPs. They told us about the challenges of politics, including the threat of personal harm, representing diverse constituents, and maintaining a non-sectarian Christian witness. We also interviewed a politician's wife, who provided insight into how political service impacted family life.

Some politicians felt their congregations supported their work; for others this was not always the case. They believed their congregations had contributed to peacemaking, to a greater or lesser degree. Some said the Presbyterian Church in Ireland (PCI) should have stood up to Paisley, or better prepared people for the changes that came after the Belfast Agreement.

They thought the churches could contribute to a better future by acknowledging victims' suffering and advocating reconciliation. But their personal definitions of reconciliation differed, underlining how challenging it is for the churches or any civic bodies to speak about it in the public sphere.

'The churches helped prevent Northern Ireland
from sliding into all-out civil war.'

Jeffrey Donaldson was raised in Kilkeel Presbyterian in Co. Down, attending Sunday School, the Boys' Brigade and youth club. At eighteen, he joined the UUP and the Ulster Defence Regiment (UDR). It was 1982, shortly after the hunger strikes by republican prisoners. 'I felt there was a dual approach to the Troubles: we had to support the democratic process, but at the same time, there was a security response.' Jeffrey was elected to the Northern Ireland Assembly in 1985. He was involved in the negotiations that produced the 1998 Belfast Agreement, but opposed it because it allowed Sinn Féin to enter government before Irish Republican Army (IRA) decommissioning. In 2004, he joined the DUP.

In 1986, Jeffrey gave a fiery speech at a Unionist meeting in Tullyhappy Orange Hall, South Armagh. 'I was at that time very clear that there was only one way to deal with terrorism, and that was with a strong security response.' After the meeting, the chairman handed him a slip of paper with '2 Chronicles 7:14' written on it, telling him this was the answer to Northern Ireland's problems. Jeffrey recognised the reference as a Bible verse. When he got home he read the verse: 'If my people, which are called by my name, shall humble themselves, and pray,

and seek my face, and turn from their wicked ways; then
will I hear from heaven, and forgive their sin, and will
heal their land.' Jeffrey said,

> I closed the Bible and put it away. But I never forgot
> that verse. Two years later when I became a Christian,
> and over a period of time, I began to understand what
> that verse really meant. It meant this is not going to
> be solved by throwing more police and soldiers at the
> problem. We must be Christ-like in our approach to
> the peace process. This means we have to sit down
> with people we never imagined we would sit down
> with.

Two of Jeffrey's cousins, police officers, were murdered
by the IRA. After the funeral of a UDR colleague, 23-year-
old Alan Johnston at Mourne Presbyterian in Kilkeel in
1988, 'I questioned myself – what if it was me and not
Alan? Where would I stand in relation to God? Things
that were happening prompted me to think about my
own mortality. The Troubles were a factor in my coming
to faith.'

Jeffrey said,

> I have no doubt whatsoever that the support provided
> by the churches during the Troubles saved lives.
> Especially in rural Ulster, where a lot of these deaths
> occurred, the support mechanisms that the church
> had in these local communities had two effects.
> One: as a support base to help people through their
> period of suffering and loss. Two: as an influence
> to persuade people that turning to violence was not
> the way. That was a safety valve within the Protestant

community that helped persuade people we had to abide by the rule of law, and that in the end, good would overcome evil.

He attended many funerals where the local minister and the Moderator urged people not to retaliate, a message that resonated beyond the church walls to the community. 'The churches helped prevent Northern Ireland from sliding into all-out civil war.'

Jeffrey is DUP spokesperson on dealing with the past. He believes reconciliation is possible and the churches can help achieve it.

My faith has been important in helping me to reach a place of healing. That's been important in my political career, because it's enabled me to engage with my enemy. As a society, we haven't yet reached a stage of healing. I feel we need to open up the past, because if we don't have recognition and acknowledgement, we will not have healing and reconciliation. Church leaders can affirm that reconciliation is not wrong, that reconciliation does not have to be about betraying the memory of a loved one.

'Our church walked away and said
it's easier not to be involved.'

Mark Neale joined the UUP in 1991 after moving to Portadown. 'David Trimble was the MP. He was young and dynamic, very involved locally and very engaging. We became friends and I got involved in politics.'

Mark's mother was Presbyterian and his policeman father was a Methodist from the Republic. When he was

young, they lived in Ballybeen Estate in Dundonald. 'In
the early 1970s there were tensions with the police. On
occasions we were under threat.' He recalled sleeping in the
rear of the house for fear of petrol bombs. When his father
was posted to Kells, Co. Antrim, people in the primarily
Protestant village were initially suspicious of his father's
southern accent. 'Being seen to be active in the Presbyterian
church helped us integrate into the community.' His father
was moved to Ballymoney, and Mark spent his formative
years there in Trinity Presbyterian. Ballymoney was
relatively quiet during the Troubles. 'Thankfully, there was
nothing to be radical about [growing up in Ballymoney].
Had I grown up in Ballybeen, I genuinely believe I could
have joined a paramilitary organisation. My mother says
the church and family would have kept me safe, but in my
own mind, I was very angry. My politics, as a young person,
was quite extreme.'

Mark's interest in politics grew during his time at
Sunderland Polytechnic. He attended a Student Union
(SU) meeting where a motion was tabled to support 'Irish
freedom' and the 'freedom fighters of the IRA'. He was
horrified. 'That was just after nine police officers were
murdered in an attack in Newry.' By this stage Mark's
mother and brothers were also members of the Royal
Ulster Constabulary (RUC), so he became active within
the SU's Representative Council and tried, successfully,
to move the SU to the 'centre' from what he saw as an
'extreme left' position. His time at college matured his
political views. 'I saw a different side of life.'

In 1996, Mark stood for election to the Northern
Ireland Forum, a body that was part of the choreography
around the political negotiations of the peace process. He
was subsequently elected to Craigavon Council in 1997.

His electoral area included Drumcree during some of the worst years of the parades dispute. The 1998 Belfast Agreement divided the UUP, but he supported it. Mark lost his seat in the 2001 elections. He worked as a special advisor for Trimble between 2002 and 2005 and for the UUP until 2007.

Mark's pro-Agreement stance put him in a difficult position with some in his First Portadown congregation. He estimated that probably 60 per cent of the congregation was against the Agreement. 'First Portadown had seen many tragedies during the Troubles and some members of the congregation found the Agreement difficult to cope with.' Others in the congregation encouraged him. 'The guys that sat beside me in the choir would have prayed for me.' His district elder visited his family and prayed with them. Mark believed his minister just didn't know what to say about politics, so there was 'very little [active] contact' with his minister on politics. He was encouraged by his uncle, Rev. Robert Lockhart of Elmwood Presbyterian in Lisburn. 'He was very good – praying for me, encouraging me, advising me.'

Mark thought some ministers in PCI, like Rev. Ken Newell, went too far down the ecumenical road. 'People perceived Ken as speaking with the authority of the Presbyterian Church, when he didn't.' He said likewise that other ministers were political, but they 'said radical pro-union things' and this wasn't helpful either. 'PCI didn't have a settled voice.' But worst of all were the Presbyterians who withdrew from public life, 'concentrating on family, on business, or getting their children out of Northern Ireland. There was a brain drain to England and the children never came back. Our church walked away and said it's easier not to be involved.'

Mark was wary about how reconciliation was being handled because 'we're a wee bit too focused on reconciling the past. What we're trying to do is justify or not justify what happened.' He said unfortunately too many people perceive reconciliation as 'attached to a liberal tradition of ecumenism'. He preferred to think about reconciliation as 'going forward with each other'. That means, 'We have to recognise what both sides did. I don't think we can reconcile the past. Reconciliation is about creating a future.'

'You can't believe you've been through it and come out the other end normal human beings.'

Gary was elected before the Troubles and served three decades as a UUP councillor. In the 1970s, he advocated, along with others, a system where unionists and nationalists would rotate the council chairmanship. His wife Lily said, 'He then got a letter from the Orange Order to say they would prefer he didn't walk on the Twelfth.' Gary's father had been an Orangeman. 'I enjoyed the crack of the lodge meetings, but it's when you grow a bit older you realise that these are the sort of organisations that tend to polarise when things go sour within communities. I was quite cross at the time. But it didn't change my view.'

Gary and Lily operated a shop, employing Catholics and Protestants and serving the whole community. It was bombed many times. Lily said, 'There were so many occasions one of us should have been killed. Bombs had gone off outside the door and we were still in the shop.' They installed a camera, 'to see if we could help catch these bombers', Lily said. The next time there was a bomb, they eagerly brought the video home. Lily said,

'The video showed a boy wheeling a pram down the street, into the doorway, and BOOM. We're sitting watching the recording later – with the children – and we were all incredulous. It's like we had screws loose – watching our own shop being blown to bits. Sometimes if you didn't laugh, you'd have cried, so it was easier to laugh.'

Lily shook her head. 'When you look back on it now, you can't believe you've been through it and come out the other end normal human beings. I think that comes from the church. You're taught it's your duty to help people, no matter who they are. That's what keeps people like us doing what we do.'

Like many councillors, Gary carried a personal protection weapon. Lily worried when he was out late at political meetings. 'What I found difficult was not knowing whether he'd left the council offices to come home and never got home; or whether he was still there. Odd nights I got out of bed and drove the car down to the council to see if his car was still there.'

While Gary was on the council, it transitioned from unionist control to a body that more accurately reflected the demographic mix of the population. 'Within the council itself, I would have tried to cool down the fire-mongers.' When asked why he kept going, he said, 'You think you're going to be able to put things to rights.' Lily added, 'I don't know why he stayed on the council or why I let him! But we were young and vibrant and bringing up a family and there was a loyalty to the community.'

People in their congregation often volunteered to help them after bombings. The minister visited regularly. Lily said, 'He was a great clergyman and would have been the first one up the street to speak to us when we'd have a bomb. He never preached retribution. His message was to turn the other cheek. There was always something in his sermons that encouraged you to be true and faithful, and things would come right in due time.'

Lily contrasted Presbyterian ministers to Rev. Ian Paisley. 'Normally Presbyterians would not have felt it right for anyone to pick up a gun or to do anything wrong to their neighbour. Whereas I felt the DUP and Paisley tended to encourage that.' Gary believed PCI should have challenged Paisley. 'They maybe didn't involve themselves strongly enough in the face of the Free Presbyterian movement. The church has had a tough time trying to compete with the Free Presbyterians. Paisley took no prisoners.'

'We were a haven for people.'

Stewart Dickson was brought up Methodist in Greenisland, a community between Belfast and Carrickfergus. The Methodist church didn't have a Boys' Brigade (BB) company, so he went to one in Greenisland Presbyterian. Eventually, joining the Presbyterians 'seemed like a sensible thing to do'. He served thirty-three years as captain of the BB and eventually became an elder.

Greenisland was predominantly Protestant until the 1960s, when a new phase of housing development attracted Catholics who had been living in poor conditions in North Belfast. 'It was peaceful and harmonious up until the Troubles started. A significant number of Catholic boys joined the Boys' Brigade. We were a very integrated community. Things took a fairly sinister turn when the Troubles started.' He recalled 'a particularly horrific incident – I don't want to describe what we all saw that day' when 'a police officer was blown up in his car by loyalists. That and other incidents started to cause tensions in the community.' Catholics began to move out, not just because of the Troubles. They missed their family support networks in North Belfast and were beginning to be intimidated by paramilitaries. 'People were burnt out of their homes or had red crosses painted on their front doors.' Stewart was sad to see them go. 'The Catholic Church has declined from a vibrant parish to the point where there's no parish priest in Greenisland any longer.'

Stewart's role in BB drew him into the local community association, where he got his start in politics. In 1977,

> A woman who had been elected to the council for the Alliance Party came up to me after one of those meetings. She said, 'You're the sort of person who would be a good councillor. Would you think of joining the Alliance Party?' At the time my parents were Ulster Unionist. It was the old rebel in me, I certainly wasn't going to become what my father was. I said, 'Yeah, that's a good idea.' It just so happens she was Catholic and it didn't make a bit of difference to me.

Stewart is still an MLA.

Stewart was encouraged by a long-time minister in his congregation, Rev. Douglas Armstrong. Douglas struck up a friendship with a local priest, Fr Tony Curran. 'They appeared on the evening news in the run up to Christmas week, Fr Tony playing his guitar and Douglas singing carols. That was big news at the time. They were very brave. There was a backlash.' The Orange Order and the Free Presbyterian Church protested outside Greenisland Presbyterian.

> I will always remember Douglas' daughter being
> extremely distressed and coming into church that
> Sunday and saying that one of the people standing
> outside holding the placards was a boy in her class
> at school. Whatever individual members of the
> congregation felt about the Troubles, that was a
> seminal moment for us. We were under attack and it
> brought us together.

Stewart also appreciated the leadership of Methodist Rev.
Harold Good, who served in Greenisland for several years;
and the principal of the Catholic school, who had a deep
faith. 'It wasn't superficial. There was stuff happening
deep down underneath in terms of developing faith,
understanding each other, sharing and praying together.'

Stewart 'didn't know' how PCI as a whole had
responded to the Troubles.

He believed his congregation 'did step up to the mark
when the Troubles got going. We were a haven for people
in terms of comfort in regular prayer, and in respect to
responding to incidents.' Other congregations were 'very
strongly Orange or Unionist'; while others withdrew from
the fray altogether. His ministers took an interest in his
political career, and supported him during difficult times,
like when his house and car were attacked, or arsonists
targeted his office during the loyalist flags protests in 2012.
'I have never felt anything other than incredibly supported.'

*'They've carried [their suffering] with great dignity and we can
pay tribute to that.'*

Danny Kennedy was a UUP politician for more than
three decades, serving as Deputy Speaker of the Northern

Ireland Assembly, Minister for Regional Development, and Minister for Employment and Learning. He lost his seat in 2017 and now works as a welfare support officer for a victims' group.

Danny was born in Bessbrook, Co. Armagh, and is a life-long member of Bessbrook Presbyterian, where he is clerk of session and Sunday School superintendent. When he was sixteen, the Kingsmills Massacre (1976) occurred a few miles from Bessbrook. Republican gunmen stopped a bus carrying twelve workmen, murdering ten and grievously injuring another. The lone Catholic was instructed to run away, escaping death. Five members of Danny's congregation were killed.

> The defining experience of the Troubles for me was the Kingsmills massacre. My parents ran the newsagents' shop and I was their chief paperboy. That brought me into contact with the people of the village. I had regular contact with nine of the ten victims. There was the enormous shock of it and the immediate aftermath: the grieving process, the funerals, and the media descending.

His memories of the funerals are vivid. 'When you see a father shake with uncontrollable grief at the loss of his only boy, it has a profound impact. The sight of so many coffins at the front of our church is an image that is like a photograph burnt in my memory.' Danny credited community leaders, including his minister, Rev. Robert Nixon, with defusing tension. 'They didn't see vengeance as the alternative. Considerable tribute is due to those people because they stood up and said: "We are going to support our families, our loved ones, our friends, but we are not going to respond with bitterness or return the evil to others."'

At the time, Danny questioned why God allowed this to happen. He did not become a committed Christian for six more years. 'You saw people suffering something so undeserved. I'm not sure that it was a reason why I didn't come to faith sooner, but it's probably in the mix of adolescence and growing up and beginning to make sense of things.'

Danny was elected for the first time in 1985, to the local council. 'Politics was tough. It was a real challenge to show the love of Christ in an angry debate. People who elect you want you to reflect their views. Sometimes that involves saying hard things.' He was often asked for public comment after killings. 'When you comment as a politician, you must be careful that you remember who is suffering here, that it's not about who can get a cheap headline. I always tried to emphasise the personal loss and the impact it would have on their lives.'

The 1998 Belfast Agreement split the UUP. Danny supported it, even though, 'The morality of '98 stinks.' For him, parts of the Agreement were immoral because prisoners were released, and the wide-ranging police reforms that followed did not recognise the police's role in restraining violence. 'Historically, the Protestant community had emphasised law and order and supporting the police. We'd heard promises from politicians and clergymen – "Someday there will be justice." But when justice came, we couldn't recognise it.'

Danny said most churches were broadly pro-Agreement, but they should have helped prepare people for the changes that were coming. 'People hadn't been conditioned for that change. So many couldn't deal with it, and consequently you had the turmoil that came with the Belfast Agreement and the subsequent divisions not only within Unionism or Protestantism but even Presbyterianism as to how it might be approached.'

Now, he hopes PCI can contribute to dealing with the past by encouraging people to tell their stories. 'Telling their story helps people to say: "I got that off my chest and now somebody else knows just how miserable this has been." I'm just really sorry for those who had to undergo suffering that nobody really knew except themselves. They've carried it with great dignity and we can pay tribute to that.'

CHAPTER 9

Those who Left Presbyterianism

Some Presbyterians responded to the Troubles by leaving their church. Rev. Ian Paisley's Free Presbyterian Church attracted many disgruntled Presbyterians who believed their own denomination was not taking a tough enough religious or political stand. Other Presbyterians thought their denomination was too timid when it came to advocating peace. Frustrated when their own efforts to promote peace were rebuffed, they too left.

It was difficult to locate people who had left Presbyterianism. Once people leave a church, they often lose contact with their former minister and friends, slipping out of the church networks that we used to find our other interviewees. In the end we spoke with four people: journalist Alex Kane, who became an atheist as a teenager but was nevertheless impressed with the Presbyterian Church in Ireland's (PCI) witness during the Troubles; a woman who was frustrated by her church's efforts to promote peace; Willie Frazer, a victims' campaigner who disagreed with PCI ministers who advocated forgiveness without repentance; and James Wilson, a former Ulster Defence Regiment (UDR) man and current grassroots peacebuilder who thought PCI failed to promote reconciliation. In Chapter 2, we also told the story of Rev. David Armstrong, who was forced to leave his congregation.

'The Presbyterian Church can hold its head up and say: We held our nerve.'

Journalist and unionist political commentator Alex Kane was raised in First Armagh. His father was clerk of session, and a member of the Orange Order and Ulster Unionist Party (UUP). Adopted at age six, Alex felt welcomed by the congregation that was so important in his parents' lives. 'Religion was never forced on me. The Sunday School teacher encouraged us to talk. Even when the Troubles were starting, they wanted us to talk about what was happening. My experience of the Presbyterian Church was a very positive one. They welcomed conversation and welcomed being challenged.'

As a teenager, Alex realised he was an atheist. 'My father said, "That's your choice." My mother said, "That's fine. I'm going to teach you to cook so that when we come back from church on Sunday we'll have lunch." The minister said, "I'd rather you honestly said you weren't coming in rather than going in just to please me or your dad."'

From a young age, Alex was aware of the connections between religion and politics. 'I always had this sense that the Presbyterian Church was the Ulster Unionist Party at prayer. I was never aware of the Presbyterian Church saying we need to hold out the hand of friendship to our Catholic neighbours. I never heard a Presbyterian minister ask: "Why is the Ulster Unionist Party so unwelcoming to Catholics?"' But Alex's father asked that question. 'My father believed in equality through Christianity. He thought the UUP and the Presbyterian Church could have done more to make Catholics feel welcome. He believed if you didn't treat people equally and with respect, you shouldn't be surprised if they turn on your faith and your politics.'

Yet Alex thought Presbyterian congregations and the Orange Order were moderating influences on young men who would have otherwise turned to paramilitarism.

> I once asked a man who joined a paramilitary group, 'How did you end up joining when some of your friends didn't?' He said, 'Two of my friends joined the Orange Order. Their parents were connected to the local Presbyterian church. My parents didn't go at all. The minister from the congregation and a couple of young men came round and got them. Nobody came and got me apart from a couple of hoods who said, "Here's a role for you." I ended up with a prison sentence and they ended up with good jobs.'

On another occasion a man told Alex, 'Your dad said something that changed my life. I was tempted to take this fight on ourselves. But he said, "No, once you take the fight yourself, you can't rely on Christ and you can't rely on your former friends. Stand your ground. Don't leave that ground and go on to a bloodier one."' Alex shared several similar stories, adding, 'I don't know if this was a deliberate policy or just people on the ground having a quiet word, asking, "Do you really want to go down that path?"'

Alex contrasted PCI and its leaders with Rev. Ian Paisley, who he regarded as 'filling people with poison. You can't call the pope the anti-Christ and then be surprised when people think you hate Catholics.' While Paisley lured many away from Presbyterianism, Alex believed this helped PCI in the long run.

Paisley was a God-send for the Presbyterian Church because he took a malign element out. It is astonishing, the number of people who went into the darkness who have connections with Paisley, maybe not through the Free Presbyterian Church but certainly through his party. Paisley saw the UUP and the Presbyterian Church as soft, woolly liberals who couldn't recognise the evils of Catholicism. Now, the Presbyterian Church can hold its head up and say: We held our nerve.

But Alex was pessimistic about Northern Ireland's future. 'People vote for the DUP [Democratic Unionist Party] or Sinn Féin because of constitutional issues. So, in that sense, there's not much the church can do.' His assessment of the prospects for reconciliation was similarly grim.

I remember a woman telling me, 'Alex, I lost two sons. I could reconcile not knowing my sons' killers if I looked round and saw a government that was working, people working together. It's like a double blow to me – my boys died in vain.' It doesn't matter if you're a Presbyterian all your life or what your religion is – if your husband or son has been killed and now you're seeing the enemy in government, that hurts. Then if you hear your church leaders saying: 'I think we should all just get together and be happy' – you can't do that. It's not possible.

'When you tried to implement anything,
you just hit a brick wall.'

Louise was raised in the conservative Brethren church. As a child she had a born-again experience. She considered herself an evangelical, but 'I couldn't understand why the Brethren felt they were the only ones that were right and would get to heaven and nobody else would.' She married a Presbyterian and began attending his church. She became increasingly convinced churches should be promoting peace. 'I've always been interested in why people are so strongly against one another. I think to myself now: Why did other people not question things? I still haven't got to the bottom of it.'

Louise attended several Presbyterian congregations in different parts of Northern Ireland. The level of interest in peace varied. At the time of the Belfast Agreement, she was part of a home Bible study group in her congregation. She recalled the first meeting after the Agreement: 'I said, "We've got to celebrate!" I even brought cheap champagne. They all looked at me as if I was crazy. Some people would have agreed with me, but I got the feeling they weren't really enthusiastic.'

Louise met like-minded people through organisations like Evangelical Contribution on Northern Ireland (ECONI) and Corrymeela. 'ECONI examined the scriptures in a way that made sense to me,' she explained. 'Everything ECONI and Corrymeela said about reconciliation was terrific in theory.' She pointed to a box of these organisations' magazines and training booklets that she had kept. 'It's all in there. People could pick it up and start again.'

In the 1990s, PCI encouraged its congregations to appoint a peace agent, a member to lead peace initiatives.

Louise became one. She developed a partnership with a Catholic parish across town. At its height, about twenty people from her congregation took part. 'We hired buses and took people back and forth. We had really good discussions. I got to know people and I was accepted by them. They wanted to be friends and we had services in their church and they came to services in ours.' Louise also attended peace-themed events organised by PCI.

> They were great for having wonderful sessions at a weekend, all day with lovely cakes. We'd sit and listen to wonderful speakers and be enthused. The minister even said to me one time: 'I hope this isn't just going to be going to a conference, we need to be doing things.' But I was doing things. I was taking people back and forth to the Catholic parish and I was writing articles in the church magazine. On the surface, it seemed to be working. Maybe it did have effects that I don't know about. But I really was a bit disillusioned at the end.

Most participants in her congregation's peace group were retired. It began to 'dwindle' as their health declined, and they could no longer attend. Around that time, Louise noticed PCI was promoting a Preparing Youth for Peace programme as part of its wider Peacemaking Programme. Excited, she approached her congregation's youth leader. 'He just shrugged. He had other ideas. That disappointed me.' Undeterred, Louise brought it to the attention of her minister and elders. 'None of them picked up on it. I never really understood why. No reason given. I would love to know if Preparing Youth for Peace worked for other congregations.'

Not long after that, Louise left PCI. She now attends
a liberal congregation in a different denomination. 'We
did a lot of talking and it all made great sense. But when
you tried to implement anything, you just hit a brick wall.'

*'Victims feel the churches are trying to force them
into forgiving them people.'*

Victims' campaigner Willie Frazer grew up in the Church
of Ireland in Whitecross, Co. Armagh. His father, a part-
time UDR man, was murdered by the Irish Republican
Army (IRA) when Willie was just fifteen. Over the next ten
years, four more members of his family were murdered.

Willie married a Presbyterian, and began attending
his wife's church, First Armagh. He remained in the
congregation for a decade. 'As the peace process went
along, I couldn't agree with the things the Presbyterian
Church were coming out with. That was one of the
reasons why I left.'

Willie objected to those in PCI who promoted
forgiveness in the absence of repentance. He thought
republicans would never repent because they still believe
IRA violence was justified.

> If some boy came into me and said: 'I killed your
> father, I was wrong, there was no justification in doing
> it, and no one could ever justify it' – I'd forgive him.
> I wouldn't go for tea with him, but I would forgive
> him and say: 'You've put my mind at rest.' But if that
> man came in to me and said: 'I killed your daddy, but
> it was for a good cause' – that's a different situation.

In 2005, Willie attended a meeting at Fitzroy Presbyterian
in Belfast where Fr Alec Reid from Clonard Monastery

and Methodist Rev. Harold Good spoke about witnessing IRA decommissioning. Willie confronted Alec, and after some angry exchanges, Alec said: 'The reality is that the nationalist community in Northern Ireland were treated almost like animals by the unionist community. They were not treated like human beings. It was like the Nazis' treatment of the Jews.'[19] Willie said,

> I felt I was sitting in a Presbyterian hall filled with several hundred people from the Protestant churches background and it was down to me to get up. It shouldn't have been my place to stand up. The church should have showed leadership there. The church should have challenged him, but they didn't. That was another reason why I fell out with the church.

Frazer attended a Free Presbyterian congregation 'for a while', but left because 'they were a bit hypocritical'. In a reference to Rev. Ian Paisley's decision to sit in government with Sinn Féin, Willie said, 'You can't stand up and say this is wrong, and then sit down with the boy who's done the wrong, and say, "It's ok, it's me that's doing it."' Willie, who died in 2019, belonged to a Pentecostal congregation at the time of our interview.

Willie remained frustrated that the churches have pressured people towards reconciliation.

> They throw this word reconciliation into it. Most victims I know, it turns them away to hear them words. When you talk about reconciliation, it comes across different to people like ourselves. It means that we are reconciling with the people who killed us. We don't need to be reconciled with the people that killed

us because we're not going to go out and kill them. But it seems the people who have been attacked are being told they need to reconcile, not the people who did the attacking. A lot of victims feel the churches are trying to force them into forgiving them people. Victims get blamed for holding up progress, but it's not the victims, it's the perpetrators.

'Post-Troubles there was no change of
culture in terms of reconciliation.'

James Wilson grew up in Trinity Presbyterian in Ballymoney. His family were long-time members: 'I come from a tradition of ruling elders and lay preachers stretching back to the 1859 Revival.' His father was a ruling elder, ran the youth club, and occasionally preached. At sixteen, James became a member. By nineteen, he was serving on the congregation committee.

In 1972, when James was still a teenager, the IRA detonated a car bomb on Main Street in Ballymoney, killing a Protestant civilian. James remembered 'the camaraderie, the sense that we're all victims in seeing our town destroyed'. The attack convinced him and his friends that they should defend their community. James initially joined the Ulster Defence Association (UDA), then a legal loyalist vigilante mass movement. Because he was underage, his father went to the UDA commander and convinced him to release him. As soon as James was old enough, he joined the UDR.

In 1975, four local members of the paramilitary group the Ulster Volunteer Force (UVF) were killed when the bomb they were transporting exploded prematurely. James recalled that a Presbyterian minister refused to bury one of them, who was just seventeen years old.

The minister openly refused to bury a terrorist. My father was very hurt by that. His words were: 'If I hadn't given you a steer, boy, it could have been you in that car.' I remember the funeral. There was two or three thousand, just a vast multitude. It wasn't in any way solidarity with the terrorism, but a sense of how dare this Presbyterian minister deny the grieving family Christian comfort. Irrespective of how he died, the family that's left is a victim of the Troubles. Here's a family that's lost their only boy and the Presbyterian Church tells them to get lost.

James said Trinity 'wasn't a serving church as such', in that only two men in it joined the UDR. His membership was looked down on. 'I was hanging around with men who drank a lot. Men whose morals might be questioned. They thought that's not where a good Christian boy should be.' Yet James 'thanked God' he joined the UDR, because the older men 'mentored me' and counselled him against taking revenge. 'It gave me a safety valve that I didn't join the paramilitaries.' As for his churchgoing, 'Well, the IRA didn't take Sundays off. So, if duty called you went and you missed church. I just shrugged my shoulders and said, it's the real world, get lost. Our patrols and checks deter terrorism.' In one memorable search operation, James' platoon uncovered a sizeable loyalist arms cache. 'The UDR is often demonised and equated with terrorists. I would challenge our critics to pause and ponder how many innocent Catholic lives we saved that day.'

During the Troubles, James perceived PCI and other denominations as 'removed' from peacemaking, citing the influence of evangelicals who taught 'a strange Troubles-related theology'. While this theology wasn't preached by his own minister, he remembered 'after-church rallies', where it was promoted. The preacher would use a text from the Old Testament which described how the Israelites were delivered from their enemies when 'they would turn again to the Lord'. James explained: 'I heard a version of that preached over and over again with this latter-day application: all you sinful people, if you come to Christ tonight, then God will keep His promise and He will deliver Ulster. Ulster was the new Israel.' He added that within PCI, there was an influential view that Christ's second coming was nigh, and that 'Christ could come tonight and take us all away from these Troubles.' On top of that, 'The Rev Ian Paisley used every opportunity to ridicule, to slander, and to verbally abuse' PCI. James recalled the Rev. David Armstrong case (Chapter 2) and said that in rural areas, there was a 'haemorrhaging' of people to Paisley's Free Presbyterian Church. 'Men who should have spoken out were silent because they didn't want to attract Free Presbyterian criticism. Free Presbyterians would have been quite happy if PCI had gone down completely and was no longer in existence.'

After a career in corporate counsel and academia, James moved across the River Bann into Co. Londonderry and joined a local Presbyterian congregation. He was active in grassroots peacebuilding. Years after the Belfast Agreement, 'I talked to my minister about doing things with Catholics – but there was that sharp intake of breath. He just couldn't see outside the box.' The loyalist flags protests of 2012 were intense in his area, with attacks on Catholic homes. James said,

I went to the Church of Ireland minister and he said, 'Yes, I'll take a stand on this.' We went down and we spent the evening at a [Catholic] home, that had been under attack. We were waiting for the windows to go in, waiting to confront whoever wanted to cause bother. The two Presbyterian ministers didn't want to know. I saw them the next day walking past, literally on the other side of the street. Gazing into empty shop windows.

James believed PCI's 'Church in the Public Square' initiative (2014–16) had promise. It was a series of discussions on social and political issues, including dealing with the past and the legacy of 1916. At one event James attended, a former UDR colleague stood up and criticised PCI for reflecting on 1916. 'It was as much as to say, "You're there to open the doors on a Sunday, you're there to preach a sermon, you're there to bury the dead, you're there to visit the sick, you're there to have Gospel services. But this is beyond your remit."' James said PCI's Council for Public Affairs 'has got backlash from it'.

But for James, those Presbyterian ministers' failure to support Catholics during the flags protests was a final straw. He now attends the Church of Ireland. The lack of response to the flags protests at the local level reflected what he believed was a wider failure on the part of PCI. 'None of the churches had a good record during the Troubles. But post-Troubles there was no change of culture in terms of reconciliation. There was no lead given. Overseas students now come to study why our peace process failed.'

CHAPTER 10

Critical Friends

We spoke with ten 'critical friends' of Presbyterianism whose positions in politics, churches or community organisations enabled them to evaluate Presbyterian responses to the Troubles. The critical friends included politicians from Sinn Féin and the Social Democratic and Labour Party (SDLP), leaders from the Catholic, Church of Ireland and Methodist churches, republican and loyalist ex-combatants, and senior civil servants.

The critical friends echo many of the criticisms made in previous chapters by Presbyterians themselves: the Presbyterian Church in Ireland (PCI) 'withdrew' from the rough and tumble of the Troubles, did not support people who were taking risks for peace, did not understand victims' needs, did not understand why loyalists turned to violence, and abandoned loyalist communities when they were most vulnerable. Yet the critical friends recognised that PCI was not alone in these shortcomings: all churches could be subjected to the same critiques. Some analysed the consequences of PCI's institutional structures: the one-year Moderatorship limits leaders' influence; and the autonomy of local ministers and congregations means that communications from the General Assembly or denominational headquarters can be rather freely embraced or ignored. Yet the critical friends also recognised the often-heroic efforts of Presbyterians who were trying to make a difference. They believed PCI – indeed all the churches – retained enough people of compassion to help build a better future.

'Let's have a remembrance day that we can do together.'

Seamus Mallon had a long and distinguished career in politics, serving as the first Deputy First Minister of Northern Ireland (1998–2001) and Deputy Leader of the SDLP (1979–2001). He was part of the SDLP's negotiations team in the talks that produced the Belfast Agreement. 'I've lived in Markethill, Co. Armagh, all my life. We've all lived here for centuries, cheek by jowl. Nobody's going away. So, we should find a way to live together in justice and peace. The problems have been identified in the Good Friday Agreement but reconciliation between the communities hasn't even started. That's an indictment on all of us.'

Seamus described living in Markethill during the Troubles as 'very harsh at times'. As SDLP spokesperson on justice, 'I was calling for reforms in policing and the Ulster Defence Regiment (UDR)', while at the same time, 'I was visiting the houses of families of those in the police and UDR who were killed.' He recalled the pain of going to visit a bereaved Presbyterian family and being turned away at the door. He attended the funeral of everyone in the village who was killed, regardless of their religion.

Seamus' Protestant neighbours quietly looked after him in difficult times.

I won't use names but at a certain point a person gave me a warning that saved my life. That I remember.

During a particularly difficult time, during one of
the strikes, a man pulled up to our house, opened
the boot of his car and brought in enough provisions
to do us for a month. I have umpteen of those type
of examples – people I treasure. It makes you all the
more angry when you see, as I have seen, people lying
in the gutter at the side of the road having been shot
dead or blown up.

He shook his head. 'I also ask myself: How in the name of
heaven do people have so much goodness and Christianity
in them to forgive people who have killed their fathers,
daughters, sons, uncles? That human spirit is something
that's inspirational. I'm not sure I would have that type of
Christianity in me. But I see it around me all the time.'

Seamus was aware that Presbyterians as well as Catholics
had been discriminated against under the penal laws. This
gave him 'empathy' for Presbyterians due to a shared,
historical experience of religious persecution. But he was
shocked that many Presbyterians he met were not aware of
this history. 'People from Presbyterian stock have somehow
clouded over the fact that they also were discriminated
against. I have no hesitation in pointing the finger at the
lack of teaching Irish history in Northern Ireland's schools,
especially the history of all sides. If we're going to solve the
problems of today, we need to be aware of the past.'

Seamus was discouraged by the political paralysis
created by the suspension of the Northern Ireland
Assembly, and by how Brexit had destabilised community
relations. 'The church leaders and people in the churches
should start breaking down some of those barriers. We
should remind each other: God is still there, and we
worship the same God. Let's get on with it.' He observed

that other countries that have emerged from conflicts have created days of remembrance that honour the perspectives of all sides. 'Let's have a remembrance day that we can do together. Then we'll start going places.'

'There wasn't the leadership I would have liked to have seen.'

Ken Bloomfield served as Permanent Secretary to Northern Ireland's short-lived 1974 power-sharing executive, Permanent Secretary for the Department of the Environment and the Department of Economic Development, head of the Northern Ireland Civil Service (1984–91), and the BBC's National Governor for Northern Ireland (1991–9). In 1997 he was appointed Northern Ireland Victims Commissioner. His 1998 report, 'We Will Remember Them', is considered seminal in debates on how to meet victims' needs. He was also a member of the Independent Commission for the Location of Victims' Remains.

Ken was baptised in the Church of England. He grew up in Belfast and went to a Presbyterian Sunday School and a Methodist cub pack. He married a Presbyterian and their children were baptised in the Presbyterian Church. He considers himself an Anglican.

Ken believed all the churches could have shown better leadership during the Troubles.

I had the impression that people were sermonising about almost anything other than what was going on around us. I would have liked to have seen much more argument from pulpits about the evil that was being done, and the moral duty to get out of it. It could have been put simply: we're all children of God and let's not forget that. There wasn't the leadership

I would have liked to have seen, although there were exceptions like Church of Ireland Archbishop Robin Eames. There wasn't any great sign of an all-Christian alliance against the dreadful things that were happening. I found that rather disappointing. If you don't get moral leadership from the churches, where is it going to come from?

Ken thought PCI's position as the largest Protestant denomination put it in a key position. 'The thinking in that church is of great importance for the rest of the community.' But PCI's diffuse and democratic structures limited its impact. 'You can't speak of the Presbyterian Church as a unity. Congregations are different and reflect the bad and the good that is going on around us. It is very much a case of what the incumbent minister chooses to do.' The Moderator's one-year term was also inhibiting. 'It's a very short time for a Moderator to make a mark as compared with someone like Eames, who was there for years. That rather diminishes the voice Presbyterians ought to have.' For him, the churches could contribute to reconciliation 'by admitting that a lot of the things we did to each other were totally wrong. In a very real sense, sinful. But we can't go on for ever and ever, thinking about that. We have to think forward as well as backwards.'

'When women can't make an impact proportionate to their gifts, surely the church loses out.'

Geraldine Smyth is a Dominican who has taught at the Irish School of Ecumenics (ISE), Trinity College Dublin, for more than two decades. She has also held leadership positions within her Order and on international ecumenical bodies.

Geraldine's first engagement with Protestants came through her family – her grandfather was Church of Ireland – and teenage social and job involvements. But her first spiritual encounter emerged after university, when she was teaching at Dominican College in Portstewart, where Catholics and Protestants prayed and studied the Bible together, and through participation in charismatic renewal meetings in Belfast and Dublin. 'None of this had political overtones for me. It was part of my own spiritual development.' When she studied for a master's at ISE, the programme included attending services and activities in churches from different traditions. She spent an enriching year participating in Christ Church Presbyterian in Dublin, and another at Fitzroy Presbyterian in Belfast. Later, Geraldine worked alongside Protestants in ISE and on the Interchurch Group on Faith and Politics, an ecumenical, cross-border group established in 1983 to analyse the relationship between churches and politics. Its efforts to promote reconciliation included a range of critical and topical publications.

Geraldine appreciated Presbyterian leaders who advocated peacemaking, including John Alderdice, May Blood, Lesley Carroll, Ray Davey, John and Rosemary Dunlop, Chris Gibson, John and Shirley Morrow, Katherine Meyer, Ken Newell and David Stevens.

I'm not saying all Presbyterians are intellectual nor should be, strictly speaking. But my impression was that it was a thinking church. It was able to incorporate difference without excluding people who might otherwise have ended up as mavericks because of their prophetic insight or convictions. I saw how Presbyterianism struggled to hold together very diverse convictions and thought patterns, through structures like the General Assembly or presbytery. I was envious of its system of participative governance – I wished my own church had something like it.

Geraldine had high hopes after PCI's Coleraine Declaration in 1990. 'It attempted to bring together and celebrate the evangelical movement of the heart alongside a critical approach to how the church was called to work in society.' She was disappointed that

> I didn't see it being lived out publicly in any consistent or dramatic way. I wanted PCI to be more visibly Biblically ecumenical as a church. I was impatient at the time with that phrase typically used to block change: 'The congregation won't wear it.' Yet, I met enough 'ordinary Presbyterians' to know that sometimes they challenged their minister. I admired that because I wouldn't have then seen so many Catholics challenging their priests on closed attitudes or stances.

Geraldine said women had often led Christian peacemaking, but PCI had not recognised their contributions in this and other areas.

> I see women who have a great loyalty to their church, but don't seem to be heard. I know women who on the eve of their ordination in the Presbyterian Church have had delegations coming to their door to remonstrate with them, that they were going against God's will. But you serve with the gifts God has given you, not with the cultural hand that somebody else wants to deal out to you. If you feel thwarted in that, you actually

feel you're being thwarted in fulfilling your call. When women can't make an impact proportionate to their gifts, surely the church loses out. All our churches have mountains to climb in that respect.

'They were Protestant clergy, so they could open doors.'

Sean Murray is an ex-prisoner, Sinn Féin policy advisor, and head of a residents' association. He grew up in the Clonard area of West Belfast. He vividly recalled the burning of Bombay Street in 1969.

When I was sixteen, extreme loyalists invaded the area and burnt it to the ground. That was my introduction to politics. I remember standing watching the houses burning and thinking, what under God is happening? A 15-year-old friend of mine was shot dead. Your priorities changed overnight from discos and football to how do I defend my family and community? That radicalised a generation.

Sean believed that none of the churches had spoken out against the injustices that fuelled the Troubles. 'The key religious establishments have to examine themselves and ask: "Did we turn a blind eye to it – discrimination, second-class citizenship, one party rule? Did we challenge it?"' While in prison, he stopped practising Catholicism, though 'I would still try and lead my life as a Christian in terms of how I respect and deal with other people.'

Sean had little awareness of the Protestant churches until the late 1980s–early 1990s, when he encountered Protestants through Frs Alec Reid and Gerry Reynolds at Clonard Monastery. Alec and Gerry organised secret talks between Sinn Féin and Protestant clergy. 'Political unionism refused to talk to republicans at that time, so it was up to civic unionism and that was the Protestant church leaders. It was a great risk to themselves because that wouldn't have been popular in their community.' For him, Presbyterian Rev. Ken Newell and Methodist Rev. Harold Good were important individuals; and latterly Presbyterian Rev. Brian Kennaway was a key dialogue partner. 'You might not even have known what denomination they came from because it didn't really matter to you. They were Protestant clergy, so they could open doors. If you wanted to talk to loyalists in relation to attacks, they were the go-to people. They also were a very important link with government agencies.'

Sean believed the partnership between Clonard Monastery and Fitzroy Presbyterian, Ken's congregation, helped transform relationships. 'People like Ken and Gerry were the people from different traditions who first broke the ice, in terms of sitting down and engaging. They made it easier for others to open a process of engagement. It was important that Clonard-Fitzroy was public. To our community, Fitzroy and Clonard were joined together at the hip and you'd have seen Ken in Clonard brave and often.'

Sean thought the churches would continue to slide into 'irrelevance' unless they could admit their past mistakes and 'open up engagement with local people'. He added, 'These comments aren't just directed towards the Presbyterian Church – they're also directed at the Catholic Church. There are some brilliant priests and some brilliant ministers, people who have had that engagement with their flock. The true read is how people lead their lives and deal with other people.'

*'During the conflict the churches closed
their doors to their own flock.'*

Rob is a loyalist ex-combatant who works in peacebuilding. 'My work brings people together to increase empathy and bust myths. When you remove the worst that people think about each other, really interesting and exciting things can happen.'

In the loyalist, working-class area where he grew up, most people felt abandoned by the churches.

> Even still you'd hear people saying: 'During the conflict the churches closed their doors to their own flock, to their own community.' The safest and easiest option was to leave it to someone else to pick up the pieces. That's part of the overall picture as to why the levels of church influence were pretty low if not non-existent when it came to providing leadership to working-class Protestant communities.

The churches in Rob's community 'have diminished significantly' and those who do attend 'are transient in so far as you see them coming in their nice cars, then going home however many miles away. You don't see them till the next Sunday.' This commuter church phenomenon was due to people moving out during the Troubles, especially if they attained jobs or education that made them middle-class.

Rob described his efforts to get local ministers involved in peacebuilding during periods of post-Belfast Agreement violence.

> I know personally of writing to ministers, going and meeting with them and asking them to get involved

in efforts to stop violence. They were very reluctant to do so. They viewed loyalists as people who were to be kept at arm's length for a whole host of reasons. I'm not sure the churches have managed to break off the stereotypical shackle that they have toward loyalists.

Rob acknowledged there has been 'improvement' in the quality and extent of engagement between Protestant churches and loyalists, but 'It would be substantially less compared to that between the Protestant churches and the nationalist/Roman Catholic community.' Rob attributed this to 'a conscious decision to reach out to the other flock', as well as 'a very conscious and considerable effort by Sinn Féin to open up dialogue with the Protestant churches'.

He still hoped PCI and the other Protestant churches could contribute to a better future. 'We haven't been able to deal with the past. But the churches have a particular vocabulary in their Bible teachings that can frame issues in the public square. They can talk about moving away from allocation of blame, and scapegoating, and revenge, and provide a non-retributive perspective on how we deal with generations of violence.'

'Church leaders can become dehumanised.'

Nicola Brady has been General Secretary of the Irish Council of Churches (ICC) and Joint Secretary to the Irish Inter-Church Meeting (IICM) since 2016, posts that make her responsible for the island's structures for ecumenical dialogue.[20] She has also worked for the Irish Catholic Bishops Conference on Justice and Peace (2008–16), which involved her in the Irish Churches Peace Project

(ICPP, see Chapter 7). 'The work we do is slow because it's based on consensus. We create spaces where you build good relationships.'

Nicola valued PCI's contributions to inter-church work. 'The Presbyterian Church is well-organised and good at running dialogue events,' she said, citing public discussions PCI has held on issues ranging from dealing with the past to welfare reform. 'We can learn from them.'

Nicola recognised PCI has been criticised for its lack of engagement with loyalism but sees signs this is changing. 'Within loyalism there's a false perception that if you look over the peace wall, the Catholic Church is affirming republican culture. It's much more complicated than that.' Nicola and other church leaders have met with loyalists. 'They have very challenging things to say to official church representatives. But they welcomed the fact we were there. We shouldn't underestimate the value of just showing up to listen to people.'

During the ICPP, Nicola organised a reflective exercise in which church leaders studied statements the churches had made during the Troubles.

> We picked out the key words and one of the most interesting learnings was that peace and reconciliation didn't really feature. It was all about non-violence. We realised that's not really defensible, from a Christian perspective. It's reactive, and utterly unambitious. People recognised that we need to be more proactively speaking about reconciliation and going out to listen to those who challenge us.

But she also believed that,

The work people do in holding together churches as institutions is often devalued. Some church leaders were more radical and people said, 'Well, all church leaders should be like that.' But if everyone was out there being radical, there would be nobody keeping the institution going and bringing others along who are not as receptive, for whatever reason. When that contribution isn't valued, church leaders can become dehumanised.

'It was very much about listen to us rather than listening to the community.'

Rev. David Campton is a Methodist minister and Superintendent of South and Central Belfast Circuit and Belfast Central Mission, a significant leadership position within Methodism. He has been active in evangelical and ecumenical efforts to promote reconciliation, such as Evangelical Contribution on Northern Ireland (ECONI) and the 4 Corners Festival.

David was baptised Presbyterian. An uncle was a Presbyterian minister and chaplain in the Orange Order. 'I grew up with a working-class Protestant identity.' His mother began taking him to Sydenham Methodist when repeated Troubles-related disruptions to the bus service in East Belfast made it difficult to attend a Presbyterian church. 'It was the closest Protestant church.' Passing the 11-plus exam was David's ticket to grammar school, which got him to Edinburgh University. 'I left Northern Ireland never intending to come back. When I came to faith in the 1980s, Christianity meant distancing yourself from the affairs of the world, including the conflict.'

David was studying biology but soon felt called to ministry in Northern Ireland. He was inspired by ECONI's

1985 founding document, 'For God and His Glory Alone'. When a person he had got to know was killed in the Enniskillen bomb (1987), 'I started thinking: what are Christians doing to make a difference?' During his training for ministry, an ECONI-style perspective 'wasn't encountered'. There was 'a very strong pietistic strand of withdrawal from the world within Northern Irish church culture', including Presbyterianism and Methodism. While this frustrated him, 'If it was not for the strong pietistic background of the churches that soaked up some of the pain, transformed it liturgically in worship, prayer, funerals and pastoral care, Northern Ireland could have been Balkanised. In many ways, pietism kept us from descending into all out chaos.'

Methodist ministers are stationed to a different congregation after a maximum of eight years, but a Presbyterian minister is 'called' by a congregation and may stay there for decades. David observed, 'With the Presbyterian call system, if the leanings of a congregation were towards pietistic evangelicalism, then they're going to call someone like that. It reinforced the loop. For someone to break out of that loop and start saying something radical, it could be very uncomfortable very quickly.'

David commended PCI's congregational peace agent programme, adding 'I'm not entirely convinced it's been as effective as it could have been.' He also recognised courageous leaders. 'But I'm a wee bit frustrated that we can pick out individuals. Why are there not more of them? Why do they stand out like a sore thumb? That's the biggest indictment of the institutions. And anything I would say about the Presbyterian Church I would say about the Methodist Church.'

He acknowledged the criticism that Protestant churches had abandoned working-class loyalist communities but stressed this was not an intentional strategy.

> If someone is saved in a working-class environment, and starts going to church, there can be personal economic benefit. A colleague of mine used to describe it as 'evangelical lift-off', because a discouragement of drinking, smoking and gambling can have a positive economic impact on a family's life. They would move up the social ladder and then move out of the area.

Congregations in working-class areas dwindled; many closed. 'There was no intention to leave, but there was no intentional engagement either and that's the problem. If there was engagement, it was very much about listen to us rather than listening to the community.'

'It's bewildering that I never encountered
a minister from a local church.'

Connor grew up in a republican family in a predominantly Protestant town. He was later a Sinn Féin politician.

> I experienced job discrimination and I encountered sectarianism. In the town where I lived, carrying a hurling stick home from training was enough to occasion harassment from the RUC [Royal Ulster Constabulary] and the UDR. I would be stopped at my front door, surrounded by UDR men with rifles. Other family members were tortured, taken to the RUC interrogation centre and shown pictures of brutal things that would be done to them and their family.

Connor no longer practices a religion. While recognising individual church leaders contributed to peacemaking, he was disappointed that the institutional churches had done so little. He felt church leaders were used by those in political power to downplay the injustices that led to violence.

> I'm not sure that the church hierarchies in any denomination have covered themselves in glory over the last thirty to forty years. Growing up, I wasn't aware of any positive influence that the churches had on anything that happened to my family. In fact, in some circumstances they seemed to exacerbate it, by not speaking out against job discrimination or persecution. The dialogue the church leaders had with the Northern Ireland Office and those in power was more important to them and informed their approaches more than any dialogue with ordinary people.

Despite Connor's many years in public service,

> There were no Presbyterian ministers who reached out to me or who I became aware of who were involved in efforts to hasten peace and promote justice. All those years growing up in a predominantly Protestant town, it's bewildering that I never encountered a minister from a local church. Would it have made a difference? I think it would have. And I'm convinced it would have been more faithful to the teachings of those churches.

Despite this, Connor said, 'In our household, Presbyterianism was actually esteemed.' This was down to the involvement of Presbyterians in the United Irish movement of the late eighteenth century.

> The values of the United Irish movement reflected Presbyterianism and also Catholicism. From my viewpoint, Presbyterianism was a tradition of radicalism, of enlightened ideas, of an affinity with ordinary people. Presbyterians were prominent in not only saving but renewing the Irish language. Those were not the pictures of Presbyterianism I saw in my lifetime. But I still have hope that people who identify with those ideals have an important part to play in transformation.

'Have [PCI] gathered the information from the people that allows them to speak on their behalf?'

Bertha McDougall is a former Northern Ireland Victims and Survivors Commissioner and is currently on the board of the Victims and Survivors Service. Previously, she was a teacher and worked on the Education for Mutual Understanding programme. In 1981 her husband Lindsay, a civil servant and police reservist, was shot on duty. 'My husband was shot in the back of the head. I was at home with my three children when there was a knock at the door. There was a policewoman and a man in plainclothes. I knew that was not a good scenario.' Lindsay was rushed to hospital but died of his injuries.

Bertha belonged to a Presbyterian congregation at the time; Lindsay was an elder.

> By the time he was out of the operating theatre my minister was at the hospital. During that period there

was so much prayer. I didn't want Lindsay to be left alone in hospital and the elders took turns to sit with him when I wasn't there. There was tremendous support by the church. You couldn't begin to describe it.

Bertha's faith helped her cope. 'People said to me, "How can God let things like that happen?" I said, "Being a Christian doesn't protect you from this. What it does give you is hope for life after death."'

Bertha's work as Commissioner included researching the experiences of other survivors. 'It was gathering information, collating it, and making recommendations to the Secretary of State.' She discovered that many survivors had not received the support of their churches. 'I did not get a positive reaction from people about the church as an institution. I would get a positive response about some individual ministers and priests.' This trend extended to all denominations. Yet people struggled to articulate what institutional churches could have done. 'When you asked people: "How should they have supported you?", I'm not sure they actually identified what they should have done.'

Bertha also spoke with representatives of church institutions. She was not always convinced they grasped the challenges of responding to survivors' needs. She thought the Presbyterian Moderator's short, one-year term prevented the office holder from making an impact on dealing with the past and other issues. She acknowledged it is difficult for institutional churches to engage with survivors.

If they want to help victims and survivors, PCI needs to be very careful and very clear about what they're doing and why they're doing it. They need to clarify if they are speaking on behalf of the church, and if they are, where are they getting the information to allow them to speak? The church is the people, so have they gathered the information from the people that allows them to speak on their behalf? Or are they speaking as the church as an institution?

*'There's a real opportunity for churches
to model extravagant generosity.'*

Trevor Williams is a former Church of Ireland Bishop of Limerick and Killaloe (2008–14). Originally from Dublin, he ministered for many years in Northern Ireland. He was chaplain at Queen's University, religious broadcasting producer for BBC Radio Ulster (1981–8), and leader of the ecumenical Corrymeela Community (1994–2003). He was also rector in parishes in Newcastle, Co. Down, and North Belfast.

Trevor said, 'During the Troubles the churches were caught up in the tension between the personal, the pastoral, and the prophetic. How prophetic can you be without finding there's no-one behind you?' Trevor was 'old enough to remember Rev. David Armstrong', and how he felt forced to leave his Presbyterian congregation after reaching out to a Catholic priest (Chapter 2). 'The Presbyterian Church was largely silent when there were opportunities to speak out. When I say Presbyterian Church, I also say my own.'

Trevor was inspired by 'prophetic' Presbyterian leaders like Revs John Dunlop, Norman Hamilton and John Morrow. 'The Presbyterian Church has thrown up some very significant leaders in terms of peacebuilding and reconciliation who were at the cutting edge of church thinking about a Christian response to the Troubles.' He recognised that these 'prophets' wouldn't have enthused wider Presbyterianism. 'Most congregations wouldn't have prioritised it.'

Trevor believed 'it's not too late' for the churches to shape public debate. 'Our construction of politics is adversarial, so you can't expect generosity from politicians. It must come from somewhere else – politicians must be set free by their electorate showing a better way. There's a real opportunity for churches to model extravagant generosity.' For him, extravagant generosity is expressed through 'a real in-depth listening and a self-imposed silence about your view while you're listening to others, until you really understand'.

Trevor witnessed many examples of extravagant generosity in Corrymeela. Once, a teenage girl requested prayers for a man who was to be sentenced to prison the next day. When later asked who he was, she said it was the man who had murdered her father. 'It may take her a lifetime to live into that prayer. But having the space and the courage to say it was a hugely generous act of love. That kind of risk, that kind of moving into the other person's experience, is what we actually need.' For him, this is crucial for dealing with the past. 'That's why Jesus said, "Love your enemies." Not because it would paper over the cracks of all divisions in the world, but because actually our enemies have a perspective to teach us that nobody else can.'

Trevor fears the churches could miss their opportunities to contribute to a better future if the 'us and them' mentality of the Troubles continues to permeate their theologies. Within the Church of Ireland, he observed that on all contentious issues, not just those related to the Troubles, there is a greater tendency in Northern Ireland to advocate division, than there is in the Republic.

> I'm thinking of the LGBT debate. There would be lobby saying that if we don't agree on the traditional approach, that would be a cause for dividing. That would be very strong in the North. In the South that would not be the case at all. So, what's different? It's at least in part the politics, social pressures, and the experience of the Troubles that influences our theology.

He thought the risk of division is even greater in Presbyterianism.

> In the Presbyterian tradition, getting the 'Word' right is important – you have to get the doctrine right and how you express it right. But when that is surrounded by a political context which defines ourselves as 'us' over against 'them', there's a great danger of that theology slipping into an 'ourselves alone' approach to having the truth. My own Biblical understanding makes me insist that despite differences, it is more important to remain together as Christians. There is a danger within the Presbyterian tradition that if we disagree, we divide. That is a major difficulty in terms of living with diversity.

CHAPTER 11

Concluding Reflections

The Troubles were a tragedy that unfolded over three long decades of violence and destruction. More than 3,500 people were murdered and a further 100,000 were injured. Countless others suffered emotional trauma and post-traumatic stress. The impact of these traumas rippled out to family and friends, impacting the whole of society, to varying degrees. The stories in this book have offered insights into the devastating human impact of the Troubles. They have demonstrated how personal faith, and the actions of ministers and local congregations, helped ordinary people as they responded to extraordinary events. They have also explored how people felt let down by their churches, expecting them to offer better pastoral support or to advocate more courageously for peace. They tell us that more than two decades after the Belfast Agreement, victims and their loved ones continue to suffer, and societal relationships remain broken.

The stories are primarily those of Presbyterians, but their impact resonates much further than this denomination. People of all backgrounds in Northern Ireland suffered – and persevered – in similar ways. While this book has been produced in partnership with the Presbyterian Church in Ireland (PCI), its purpose has not been to claim that Presbyterians have had a monopoly on suffering or that their responses have been in any way superior to those of others. This book has simply been an attempt to share the diversity of Presbyterian experiences of the Troubles with a wider audience, to prompt reflection on the horror of violence, and – without attempting to claim a moral high ground for Presbyterians – to extend an invitation to everyone on this island to *consider grace.*

The anger, sadness, and pain that fill these pages should leave us in no doubt that considering grace, let alone extending it to others who have wronged you, is among the most challenging of human endeavours. Yet we have also told the stories of people who have extended grace to those who have harmed them, above and beyond what could be expected in their circumstances. Even though we did not ask people directly about forgiveness, a majority, including almost all victims, introduced it into our conversations. Forgiveness, they confirmed, is not forgetting. Forgiveness always includes remembering. For them, the ultimate expression of grace is remembering in a way that helps create a better future.

Gracious Remembering

The Junction, a community relations centre in Londonderry/Derry, has an 'Ethical and Shared Remembering' programme, designed to inform commemorations of the centenaries of events that took place in Ireland between 1912 and 1922. For Methodist theologian Rev. Johnston McMaster, who helped develop the programme, ethical and shared remembering includes pondering the human cost of violence and giving victims a public voice so we can really understand how violence has affected them. It means asking what got us to a point where we resorted to violence and reflecting on how we justified it. It includes the capacity to be self-critical about our own and our community's actions; and to listen to alternative perspectives on and interpretations of the same events.[21]

Ethical and shared remembering is a laudable pursuit. It is probably not possible without grace, as defined in the opening chapter of this book: free and unmerited favour, extended to those who do not deserve it; or courteous good will. The stories in this book have convinced us that grace is a gift, one that individuals can receive from others, themselves, or God; grace is also a gift that individuals and communities can bestow on each other.

The stories in this book go some way towards a Presbyterian contribution to a gracious remembering of the Troubles. These stories create opportunities for graciousness because they allow victims to be heard. We do not challenge our storytellers' interpretations of events and institutions, allowing their perspectives to stand. Absorbing people's stories is a necessary part of listening graciously. At other times, the stories are critical of the actions of PCI, some of its ministers and congregations, and of others within wider Protestantism. Some said churches as institutions had abdicated responsibility for peacemaking during the Troubles. Others said that post-Agreement, the churches continued to abdicate responsibility for contributing to victims' healing and for promoting better societal relationships. Part of PCI's commitment to a gracious remembering means listening to the pain in those stories. It also means recognising that the perceived failures of church institutions may, indeed, need to be publicly acknowledged and forgiven.

The book does not present a wide range of alternative perspectives on the Troubles, particularly Catholic ones – although these are not entirely absent. We were also struck by how often Presbyterians shared with us the kindness of their Catholic neighbours, whether it was through providing comfort in bereavement, giving them warnings that saved their lives, or praying for them. This book provides another set of perspectives on the Troubles which sit alongside many others. For gracious remembering to be 'ethical and shared', we must be mindful of other stories elsewhere, and always ask ourselves how others might see these events or if there are other interpretations that we have overlooked.

Remembering in the Present – Lament

McMaster has written that what we remember 'are interpretations of history determined not by past facts but present needs and usually through a current ideological filtering of historical events'.[22] The stories in this book have taught us that many ordinary people remember the Troubles today, and every day, and their memories hurt. Their painful memories are regularly relived in a post-conflict society where there have been few prosecutions, no truth commissions, nor even a full implementation of the recommendations of public consultations on addressing the legacy of the past. Individuals and communities have devised their own means of remembering. People in this book have told us about some of these: Remembrance Day services, marking anniversaries, plaques, and even thinking of their loved ones at the first sign of the daffodils in spring. We are also aware that remembrance can foster bitterness rather than healing or glorify and justify the violence of the Troubles.

Even before the chaos created by Brexit and the suspension of the Northern Ireland Assembly, politicians struggled to agree on how to address the legacy of the past. Most victims we spoke with felt their pain had not been adequately recognised either at an official state level or in their local communities. Others feared the dominant political parties were constructing self-serving versions of history that left no room for alternative perspectives. People also recognised that Brexit had damaged relationships on the island of Ireland and between Ireland and Britain, making addressing the legacy of the past much more difficult.

The stories in this book suggest that one way we might begin to remember in the present is to recognise our shared suffering and to respond to it with lament. Lament has been defined as a passionate expression of grief or sorrow. It is a common practice in the Hebrew Bible, including the book of Lamentations and the psalms. In fact, many psalms of lament conclude with hopelessness and despair. As David Stevens, a Presbyterian who served as leader of Corrymeela and General Secretary of the Irish Council of Churches, observed:[23]

We may need to lament and grieve for what has been lost and done, and acknowledge anger, injustice, bitterness, pain, resentment, disorientation, loss of identity and uncertainty. For this we need a language; feelings need to be released into words. The resources available in the Biblical language of lament – which found expression in the corporate grieving connected with the destruction of Jerusalem and exile in Babylon

– and the ritual actions of the faith community could be of help in this.

Rev. John Dunlop, a former Moderator of PCI, compares this to the Biblical 'valley of the shadow of death':[24]

We find ourselves in what the psalmist called the valley of the shadow of death. ... the way of suffering, grief and loss. [It] is a terrain we all must travel at some point in this life, when we lose someone we love, or we accompany others who are dying, or when we travel that road ourselves. Loss is woven into the fabric of life.

McMaster also observes that in the face of loss,

the anger or rage may be against people or it may be against God. Popular religion and piety has conditioned many to believe that anger and rage against God is wrong or is a lack of faith. In Israel's experience and understanding, not to express anger and rage towards God was the real lack of faith. The Jewish tradition has always had and still has this liberating ability to argue with God, make accusation and complaint.[25]

Similarly, Dunlop has emphasised the need to create space for 'grieving':[26]

All successfully travelled journeys of grief involve remembering, grieving and hoping. The only way to avoid the possibility of grief is to avoid the opportunities to love. It is not possible for individuals to draw a line under their loss and get on with life as if nothing has happened. It would be callous for a community to travel into the future and leave grieving people behind.

In other words, the practice of lamentation can create space for hopelessness and despair, allowing people to express their pain, trauma, and even longing for vengeance. If those normal human emotions are suppressed, they may burst out later in more destructive ways, in, for example, 'collective apathy, social paralysis or internal/external violence'.[27]

We cannot expect people to move quickly and uniformly from lament to healing, to forgiveness, to a grace-filled future. But the stories in this book have demonstrated that even as society has become relatively peaceful and some individuals have journeyed towards healing, grief and sorrow persist alongside and as an undercurrent to everyday life. The temptation is often to push people towards healing, forgiveness and reconciliation. But the challenge is to recognise that within communities, congregations, or even within a single individual, a range of complex emotions exist all at once. Being honest about this requires us to give grief its place and to create space for lament. PCI, in partnership with other churches, is well-placed to advocate for this ancient and therapeutic practice, in whatever varied forms it might take, Christian or secular.

Remembering for the Future – Considering Grace

Not all who consider grace in the face of suffering will extend it; nor will all those who seek grace have it bestowed upon them. The stories in this book have confirmed this. Yet the stories have also revealed a longing for a better future, and a deep desire that future generations should not endure more Troubles. In fact, some people made sense of what happened to them during the Troubles by telling us that they or their loved ones suffered so their children and grandchildren could live in peace.

These stories also confirmed that people will not forget their troubled past, nor should they be expected or commanded to do so. Even those who have forgiven those who harmed them continue to remember. But we could say that they are 'remembering *for* the future', or remembering in such a way that they are creating opportunities for the future to be filled with grace rather than pain. Janet Morris, a Presbyterian who lectures at Belfast Bible College, has argued that forgiveness can function as a form of 'good remembering', precisely because it acknowledges the pains of the past:[28]

> Bad or unhealthy remembering is the kind which broods over the wrongs suffered, stoking up hatred of the other and refusing to look at any possible wrong in the self, or any interpretation of events but one's own. This will harm the 'rememberer'. However, good remembering is a realistic and healthy way of dealing with the hurts of the past. In this, nothing is denied or frozen into repression; feelings and actions are acknowledged, but choices are made not to be bound by them – to absorb them and move on, open to the possibility of restoration and a new future.

She goes on to describe forgiveness as a grace which is orientated towards the future:[29]

Forgiveness can never be demanded. Only harm will come from trying to coerce people into it: it is a gift which can be given or received only in freedom. ... It is a journey, a process which demands honesty, realism and hard work – and the acceptance that some situations will not be healed in this life. ... It involves risk and vulnerability, but it holds within itself the possibility of breaking the destructive cycles of past conflict, of bringing healing to deep wounds and new life to damaged relationships.

Similarly, Nicola Brady, General Secretary of the Irish Council of Churches, has discovered that an orientation towards the future is an empowering way to shape conversations about forgiveness and remembering:[30]

When I have researched case studies where people from churches have provided transformational leadership in communities it has involved having the courage to ask the difficult questions and listen respectfully to the answers in all their painful complexity. And often what they tell me is that the question that moves people on is not about forgiveness – directly – but it's: what kind of future do you want to give to your children? But you can't go straight to that question. You've got to earn that right.

In other words, when people are asked to create a vision of a grace-filled future, they can then begin to work back from there to broach topics like healing, forgiveness and reconciliation. They begin to remember *for* the future, opening themselves up to previously unimagined possibilities.

One such possibility is reconciliation, an idea we considered so important that we asked every person we interviewed about it. We discovered as many different definitions and perspectives on reconciliation as there were interviewees. Some embraced it wholeheartedly as a Christian concept that should be promoted at individual, societal and political levels. Others thought the term should be avoided because it had become too politicised; or because they simply deemed it impossible to achieve for all individuals or at societal and political levels. Some suggested we strive for achieving respect and tolerance instead of pressurising people to reconcile. One of us (Gladys Ganiel) has previously argued that while public and political discourses about reconciliation have often been confusing and divisive, there is still much of value in the theologies of reconciliation that were developed during the Troubles. A problem is that the main insights of these theologies have been lost or have not been effectively communicated, including the idea that at its heart, reconciliation is about 'transforming relationships'.[31] But given the ambiguity and even suspicion about this word, it is neither gracious nor wise to conclude that the term reconciliation is the only or best gateway into remembering for the future, although it may be a powerful incentive for some.

In that light, we conclude by recalling PCI's Vision for Society statement, which also recognises the centrality of human relationships for 'a broken and divided world'. It reminds Presbyterians that they are 'called by God to grace-filled relationships'. Given that grace is a gift that individuals and communities can bestow on each other, we once again extend our invitation to *consider grace*, alongside all those who are already on this most painful and difficult journey. As Morris reminds us, 'grace [is] a recognition of the ongoing work of God in the lives of ourselves and others, working in places where we cannot, surprising us with unexpected gifts'.[32]

Afterword

Alan McBride's life changed forever when the IRA murdered his wife and father-in-law in the bomb attack at Frizzell's Fish Shop on the Shankill Road in 1993. His response to the bomb was initially one of anger but as the years have passed, he has come to view the Troubles as a great tragedy which could have been prevented if only people would agree to live and let live.

Today Alan is an avid peace campaigner and manager of the WAVE Trauma Centre in Belfast. He also has worked with the YMCA, was a founding member of Healing through Remembering, and served on the Northern Ireland Human Rights Commission (2012-18).

He was brought up in Antrim Road Baptist Church but these days worships at Bloomfield Presbyterian Church, in the east of the city where he now lives alone. He has one daughter Zoe from his first marriage.

'God judged it better to produce "good" from "evil" than to suffer no evil to exist.' I have no idea who said those words but I do recall coming across them in a book I was reading shortly after my wife, Sharon, was killed. They had such a profound impact on me that I had them written in graffiti onto the wall of the YMCA in Lisburn, in huge letters, by some of the young people I was working with.

The year was 1994; not long after the first IRA ceasefire and only six months on from the bomb attack on Frizzell's fish shop on the Shankill Road in Belfast. My head was all over the place as I desperately searched for meaning amidst the carnage of that day and the subsequent weeks and months that followed. This quote spoke to my soul in ways that other attempts at finding meaning had failed to do; be it the numerous conversations I had with friends and family, dozens of psychotherapeutic sessions or endless Sunday morning sermons at church.

I never did find 'meaning' because sometimes there isn't any 'meaning' to be found. Nothing that could explain away the hurt and the pain and nothing that would ever make what happened on the Shankill Road that October day to be 'okay'. To be honest, I now think I was a bit mad in the head for searching for it in the first place, but I just wanted life to be good again. I thought 'if only I could believe that Sharon's death meant something', then I could come to terms with it and 'move on'.

That was over twenty-five years ago and I think I can truthfully say I have moved on. Life is 'good' again. God is producing something good out of something that was horrible and hard. Sharon's death was still a senseless killing. They all were. All of those killed in the 'Troubles' and all of those who have died since; the latest statistic being the journalist Lyra McKee.

'Senseless killing' is my starting point. It is the quest to make the 'last one' the 'last one', which motivates me to keep going. I know and respect that different people cope in different ways with violent conflict. There are those who want revenge and those who are quick to offer forgiveness. There are those whose lives spiral downwards and those who use the trauma of what happened to rise up and make a difference.

Considering Grace has brought a collection of these individuals together and shone a light on the role Christian faith played in shaping responses to the 'Troubles'. Many of those interviewed talk of the support they received from their local church, whilst others say they felt 'abandoned' and even contemplated giving up on God. 'Why me, Lord?' is a common theme amongst those who were interviewed. One respondent, Judy, acknowledged how the faith of her husband, Ben, was shattered when he lost his parents and another relative in a single incident. Judy describes how he would 'go out in the middle of the night and sit by the grave with a cigarette'. Ben's attitude was 'there's no God to let a tragedy like that happen'.

Another, Samuel Malcolmson, believed in 'Christian ideals' but would question whether God has an actual plan. Sam was seriously injured while on duty as a serving policeman. His mother died when she heard the news. Sam criticised the church for 'being silent about victims'. He cited the example of a Presbyterian minister from Londonderry referring to Sinn Féin's Martin McGuinness 'as a Saint, or words to that effect', as being 'damaging' to victims and their families.

Whilst some fell away, others learned to lean on God, seeing their faith strengthened. I was encouraged to read Janet's account of praying to God in the aftermath of a car bomb attack on her husband, John. She described it as 'a really good time because you were so close to God … you felt you could have reached out and touched him'. Prayer was mentioned many times in the book. 'Ruth', the wife of a murdered policeman, pointed out that it was 'constant prayer' that got her through it. She explained, 'I prayed when I was out in the car, when I was peeling the potatoes *and* when I was cleaning the house.' Ruth was a disciple of Jesus before her husband died, studying the bible every day, but after the incident she found it hard to concentrate. Her faith sustained her through prayer; she pointed out that 'when you were praying, it was like you were talking to your best friend. Maybe you didn't get an answer straight away, but you knew that somebody was listening.'

Considering Grace is packed with stories such as these; stories of normal people, Christians, churchgoers and those with a mere passing interest in the teachings of Christ. I have read the accounts of victims and members of the security forces, emergency responders and health care workers, ministers, politicians and those involved in peacebuilding. As you would expect from such an eclectic mix of people, there is no 'one way' that we can collectively deal with the hurt and pain of the past. But these stories point me toward an emerging consensus that I believe could provide the scaffolding for our thinking as we move forward together.

First of all; killing is senseless. It was the starting point for my own journey and I found it reiterated time and time again as I explored the stories behind the headlines. This was best summed up by one minister, who served in both rural and urban areas of Northern Ireland, when he described it as 'meaningless, meaningless', reminiscent of the prayer of Solomon in the book of Ecclesiastes. He went on to acknowledge that all he had to offer the widow whose husband was shot dead was his tears. It would be my belief that there was comfort in those tears, and that being 'real' with those who were hurting was better than coldly quoting a verse of scripture.

Secondly; don't put the burden of 'forgiveness' onto victims and survivors who are already hurting. I understand that I might be at odds with the teachings of Jesus Christ, who asked us to 'pray for our enemies and forgive those who hurt us'. But if the focus of this book is to hear from those who have been impacted by the Troubles and to chart away forward, then we must be sympathetic to the experiences of others. Forgiveness is a good destination but it can be an impossible starting point for some people. Perhaps the question for people of faith is how to show the love of Christ to those who are hurting.

Thirdly, and in keeping with my affiliation with Presbyterianism, my final point; peacebuilding is always done best under the radar. This point was made by Lindsay Conway but endorsed by countless others under the title 'Quiet Peacemakers'. Lindsay highlighted several Presbyterian giants of peacebuilding: Ray Davey, John Dunlop and Ken Newell. There is no doubt the PCI and Northern Ireland more widely has benefitted from their work, but Lindsay makes the point, 'If we'd made a resolution in the 1980s or 90s that every Presbyterian congregation had to twin with a Catholic congregation, there would have been absolute mayhem.'

The Church has come a long way since those days, and I am pleased to say that, at least as far as inter-church work goes, it is doing better than some predicted. Of course, there is no room for complacency as there is always more that can be done, and sometimes it's okay to take a sideways glance to see how we are doing. *Considering Grace* is that sideways glance. It would be my prayer for everyone who pores over the pages of the book that lessons can be learned and a new pathway to peace and shared living forged. Perhaps, then, more of us will see and understand that in the wisdom of the almighty, producing 'good' from 'evil' was judged to be better than banishing evil altogether.

Alan McBride
August 2019

Endnotes

1   We interviewed 122 people, but two withdrew consent for publication.

2   S. Bruce, *God Save Ulster: The Religion and Politics of Paisleyism* (Oxford: Oxford University Press, 1986), p. 249.

3   D. Cooke, *Persecuting Zeal: A Portrait of Ian Paisley* (Dingle, Co. Kerry: Brandon Books, 1996), p. 79.

4   Bruce, *God Save Ulster*, p. 249.

5   G. Ganiel, *Evangelicalism and Conflict in Northern Ireland* (New York: Palgrave, 2008); C. Mitchell and Gladys Ganiel, *Evangelical Journeys: Choice and Change in a Northern Irish Religious Subculture* (Dublin: UCD Press, 2011).

6   C. Mitchell and J. Tilley, 'Disaggregating Conservative Protestant Groups in Northern Ireland: Overlapping Categories and the Importance of a Born-Again Self-Identification', *Journal for the Scientific Study of Religion* 8(4), pp. 738–52.

7   PCI, Vision for Society statement, 2016, https://www.presbyterianireland.org/Utility/About-Us/Statements/Vision-for-Society-Statement.aspx, accessed 24 May 2019. The full text is available in the appendix.

8   J. Brewer, G. Higgins and F. Teeney, *Religion, Civil Society and Peace in Northern Ireland* (Oxford: Oxford University Press, 2011). Brewer was the main author, assisted by Higgins and Teeney.

9   PCI, Coleraine Declaration, 1990, https://www.presbyterianireland.org/Utility/About-Us/Statements/Coleraine-Declaration.aspx, accessed 24 May 2019.

10 J. Dunlop, *A Precarious Belonging: Presbyterians and the Conflict in Ireland* (Belfast: Blackstaff Press, 1995), p. 125.

11 Many people could be placed in more than one category.

12 P. Grant, *Rhetoric and Violence in Northern Ireland 1968–1998: Hardened to Death* (London: Palgrave, 2001), p. 127.

13 The General Assembly approved women's ordination in 1973.

14 T. Macauley, *Little House on the Peace Line: Living and Working as a Pacifist on Belfast's Murder Mile* (Belfast: Blackstaff, 2017).

15 In 2019, there were 125 congregational peace agents, with 103 in Northern Ireland (out of 438 congregations, or 24 per cent) and 22 in the Republic (out of 98 congregations, or 22 per cent). Figures are not available for peace agents during the Peacemaking Programme, but a 2006 General Assembly report refers to more than 150 peace agents attending a conference.

16 Ganiel, *Evangelicalism and Conflict in Northern Ireland*; Brewer, Higgins and Teeney, *Religion, Civil Society and Peace in Northern Ireland*.

17 See G. Ganiel, *Unity Pilgrim: The Life of Fr Gerry Reynolds, CSsR* (Dundalk: Redemptorist Communications, 2019), pp. 205–9.

18 A dispute about a contested Orange Order parade in North Belfast. For more than three years (2013–16), people who believed Orangemen should have the right to walk home past a nationalist area maintained a protest camp at Twaddell Roundabout.

19 BBC News, 'Unionist Anger over Nazi Remarks', 13 October 2005, http://news.bbc.co.uk/1/hi/northern_ireland/4337068. stm, accessed 24 May 2019. See also K. Newell, *Captured by a Vision* (Belfast: Colourpoint, 2016), p. 239 and Ganiel, *Unity Pilgrim*, pp. 228–30.

20 The ICC, founded in 1922, is an ecumenical body that includes many of the island's Protestant churches, including the Church of Ireland, Presbyterian and Methodist. The IICM, founded in 1973, is a forum between the ICC and the Catholic Church.

21 J. McMaster, *Overcoming Violence: Dismantling an Irish History and Theology – An Alternative Vision* (Dublin: Columba, 2012).

22 J. McMaster, 'Ethical Remembering: Commemoration in a New Context', document prepared for the Education for Reconciliation Programme (Belfast and Dublin: the Irish School of Ecumenics, 2007).

23 D. Stevens, *The Land of Unlikeness: Explorations into Reconciliation* (Dublin: Columba, 2004), pp. 107–8.

24 J. Dunlop, Address at the funeral of May Stevens, Cooke Centenary Presbyterian Church, Belfast, 20 February 2018.

25 J. McMaster, 'Healing the Hurts, Shaping the Future: A Series of Six Bible Studies' (Belfast: The Methodist Church in Ireland, 2006), p. 18, https://www.irishmethodist.org/sites/default/files/pdf/issues/healingthehurtsbiblestudies.pdf, accessed 24 May 2019.

26 Dunlop, *A Precarious Belonging*, pp. 126–7.

27 McMaster, 'Healing the Hurts', p. 18.

28 J. Morris, 'Forgiveness and the Individual', Forgiveness Papers No. 11 (Belfast: Contemporary Christianity/Evangelical Contribution on Northern Ireland, 2002), p. 7, http://www.contemporarychristianity.net/resources/pdfs/Forgiveness_Paper_11.pdf, accessed 24 May 2019.

29 Morris, 'Forgiveness and the Individual', p. 8.

30 N. Brady, 'Reflections on Scandalous Forgiveness', Address at 4 Corners Festival, Clonard Monastery, Belfast, 10 February 2019. The 4 Corners Festival is an ecumenical Christian festival.

31 G. Ganiel, 'Can Churches Contribute to Post-Violence Reconciliation and Reconstruction? Insights and Applications from Northern Ireland'. In Wolffe, J. (ed.), *Irish Religious Conflict in Comparative Perspective: Catholics, Protestants and Muslims* (Basingstoke: Palgrave, 2014), pp. 59–75.

32 Morris, 'Forgiveness and the Individual', p. 8.

Bibliography

BBC News, 'Unionist Anger over Nazi Remarks', 13 October 2005, http://news.bbc.co.uk/1/hi/northern_ireland/4337068.stm, accessed 24 May 2019.

Brady, N., 'Reflections on Scandalous Forgiveness', Address at 4 Corners Festival, Clonard Monastery, Belfast, 10 February 2019.

Brewer, J., Higgins, G. and Teeney, F., *Religion, Civil Society and Peace in Northern Ireland* (Oxford: Oxford University Press, 2011).

Bruce, S., *God Save Ulster: The Religion and Politics of Paisleyism* (Oxford: Oxford University Press, 1986).

Cooke, D., *Persecuting Zeal: A Portrait of Ian Paisley* (Dingle, Co. Kerry: Brandon Books, 1996).

Dunlop, J., Address at the funeral of May Stevens, Cooke Centenary Presbyterian Church, Belfast, 20 February 2018.

Dunlop, J., *A Precarious Belonging: Presbyterians and the Conflict in Ireland* (Belfast: Blackstaff Press, 1995).

Ganiel, G., *Evangelicalism and Conflict in Northern Ireland* (New York: Palgrave, 2008).

Ganiel, G., 'Can Churches Contribute to Post-Violence Reconciliation and Reconstruction? Insights and Applications from Northern Ireland'. In Wolffe, J. (ed.), *Irish Religious Conflict in Comparative Perspective: Catholics, Protestants and Muslims* (Basingstoke: Palgrave, 2014), pp. 59–75.

Ganiel, G., *Unity Pilgrim: The Life of Fr Gerry Reynolds, CSsR* (Dundalk: Redemptorist Communications, 2019).

Grant, P., *Rhetoric and Violence in Northern Ireland 1968–1998: Hardened to Death* (London: Palgrave, 2001).

Macauley, T., *Little House on the Peace Line: Living and Working as a Pacifist on Belfast's Murder Mile* (Belfast: Blackstaff, 2017).

McMaster, J., 'Healing the Hurts, Shaping the Future: A Series of Six Bible Studies' (Belfast: The Methodist Church in Ireland, 2006), https://www.irishmethodist.org/sites/default/files/pdf/issues/healingthehurtsbiblestudies.pdf, accessed 24 May 2019.

McMaster, J., *Overcoming Violence: Dismantling an Irish History and Theology – An Alternative Vision* (Dublin: Columba, 2012).

Mitchell, C. and Ganiel, G., *Evangelical Journeys: Choice and Change in a Northern Irish Religious Subculture* (Dublin: UCD Press, 2011).

Mitchell, C. and Tilley, J. 'Disaggregating Conservative Protestant Groups in Northern Ireland: Overlapping Categories and the Importance of a Born-Again Self-Identification', *Journal for the Scientific Study of Religion* 8(4), pp. 738–52.

Morris, J., 'Forgiveness and the Individual', Forgiveness Papers No. 11 (Belfast: Contemporary Christianity/Evangelical Contribution on Northern Ireland, 2002), http://www.contemporarychristianity.net/resources/pdfs/Forgiveness_Paper_11.pdf, accessed 24 May 2019.

Newell, K., *Captured by a Vision* (Belfast: Colourpoint, 2016).

PCI, Coleraine Declaration, 1990, https://www.presbyterianireland.org/Utility/About-Us/Statements/Coleraine-Declaration.aspx, accessed 24 May 2019.

PCI, Vision for Society statement, 2016, https://www.presbyterianireland.org/Utility/About-Us/Statements/Vision-for-Society-Statement.aspx, accessed 24 May 2019.

Stevens, D., *The Land of Unlikeness: Explorations into Reconciliation* (Dublin: Columba, 2004).

Presbyterian Church in Ireland's 'Vision for Society' Statement

WE, MEMBERS OF THE PRESBYTERIAN
CHURCH IN IRELAND,
saved by grace
and called by God to grace-filled relationships,
in the power of the Holy Spirit
as ambassadors of Christ's Kingdom
in a broken and divided world;

BELIEVE that the Good News of Jesus Christ
challenges and equips us
to develop radically new attitudes and relationships
with our neighbours throughout the whole of Ireland.

WE CONFESS our failure
to live as Biblically faithful Christian peacebuilders
and to promote the counter culture of Jesus
in a society where cultures clash.

ACCORDINGLY, WE AFFIRM Christian peacebuilding
to be part of Christian discipleship
and reassert the Church's calling
to pursue a peaceful and just society in our day

WE SEEK a more reconciled community
at peace with each other,
where friend and foe,
working together for the common good,
can experience healing
and the grace of our Lord Jesus Christ.